FROM B.A. TO
PAYDAY

FROM B.A. TO PAYDAY

LAUNCHING YOUR CAREER AFTER COLLEGE

D.A. HAYDEN + MICHAEL WILDER

Stewart, Tabori & Chang
New York

Published in 2008 by Stewart, Tabori & Chang
An imprint of Harry N. Abrams, Inc.

Library of Congress Cataloging-in-Publication Data:
Hayden, D. A.
From B.A. to payday: launching your career after college / by D. A. Hayden
and Michael Wilder.
    p. cm.
 ISBN 978-1-58479-711-1
1. Job hunting. 2. College graduates—Employment. 3. Job interviews.
4. School-to-work transition. I. Wilder, Michael. II. Title.
 HF5382.7.H398 2008
 650.14--dc22
                              2008012092

Editor: Kristen Latta
Designer: Alissa Faden
Production Manager: Tina Cameron

The text of this book was composed in Info and Colossalis.

Printed and bound in the United States of America.
10 9 8 7 6 5 4 3 2 1

harry n. abrams, inc.
a subsidiary of La Martinière Groupe
115 West 18th Street
New York, NY 10011
www.hnabooks.com

THIS BOOK IS DEDICATED TO Sister Eileen O'Gorman, R.S.C.J., who taught me the importance of writing and clear expression; to Ann C. Hunt, my first boss, mentor, and "big sister," who has always encouraged me to go out on my own; and to my mother, Grace McWilliams Hayden, who, each day, exhibits the love, warmth, talent, courage, and strength I've admired all my life.

—D.A.

THIS BOOK IS DEDICATED TO my daughter Isabel, who proves to me, on a daily basis, how much I have to learn about her generation, and who, in the gentlest possible way, reminds me not to always think like a grown-up.

—Michael

CONTENTS

INTRODUCTION

"Why did my parents spend $200,000 on my college education when I can't find a job?"

"I asked if it would be okay if I moved back home after college. I said it would just be for a little while, until I figured out what I want to do. It's been eight months."

"I posted my resume on Monster, but nobody's contacting me. What's going on?"

"I've had lots of interviews but I never seem to make it past the first round. Why doesn't anyone want to hire me?"

Sound familiar? Baby boomer parents have watched over, guided, coddled, coached, engineered, and examined every aspect of their children's lives, and not a cocktail party or a business lunch goes by without discussion of the latest challenge facing or recently overcome by them. And now, as these young people begin to enter the workforce for the first time, they have a lot of new questions, concerns, and, of course, worries.

We all know kids who have friends who have been coached to get into the right preschool, kindergarten, or Montessori program. Maybe you've been one of them. They've probably had tutors to keep them ahead in their studies and they've taken focused lessons in dance, music, language, and sports. Some of these kids were coached to get into the right private secondary school. They've participated in SAT prep classes and worked with counselors to identify and secure coveted spots in the best colleges or universities. (Only in this day and age can a parent, without any sense of irony, lament—as we once heard—that their talented high-school-age son is "just another all-star soccer player who speaks Mandarin and plays the bass violin.")

You've probably noticed that throughout their lives, the millennial generation has traveled, worked, played, and partied in groups. The pack mentality applies to everything and includes high school homework groups, prom dates (and dating in general), academic group projects in college, off-campus group housing, group travel on spring break, and participation in online social networks—the ultimate group. Very few students are comfortable separating from the pack, and frankly, very few have the courage to go it alone. It's counterintuitive. Interdependence is how today's young adults think of their lives. Why separate from the pack? It's way too uncomfortable.

As the packs of millennials grow up, in college these young adults might have continued to have special tutors, mentors, and coaches. They've probably completed internships and traveled to study abroad. And they've been geared, guided, and goaded to success every step of the way.

Then they graduate and have to find a job. All by themselves.

College career services departments, with their limited resources and lack of accountability, are less equipped than ever to manage the velocity of students looking for the type of focused, one-on-one help they have been accustomed to receiving. Parents and students are left exasperated, annoyed, and directionless. Our experience with clients tells us that the frustration with career services is only escalating; many of our clients have avoided the department entirely.

Throughout their lives, this generation of young people have been able to turn to their parents when facing a serious challenge. In turn, parents likely have always been able to turn to their professional experts—tutors, music teachers, coaches—who could help their kids overcome obstacles and succeed.

But now, at the moment when they should be most prepared—graduation from college—these young men and women are suddenly facing the biggest competitive challenge of their lives. That's where we come in.

If college career services is a gymnasium, we are personal trainers.

We founded Hayden-Wilder to counsel entry-level candidates and help them create their own individual, compelling brand stories to set them apart from the competition so they can get their first jobs.

Competition for those entry-level jobs is stronger than ever. Every year in the United States alone:

- 1.4 million students graduate from college;
- less than 30 percent of college graduates get jobs through campus recruiting;
- 57 percent of college graduates move home;
- 85 percent of college graduates are not prepared to interview for a job;
- by 2008, the number of college graduate job seekers will exceed the number of jobs available by 25 percent.

As marketers who have worked with clients in every major business sector—from financial services to consumer products and health care to high-tech—we understand that a job search is essentially a marketing effort, a clear story, an understanding of the target audience, and a communications plan to deliver the message.

This book, geared to college juniors, seniors, and recent graduates, will help with that marketing effort.

First, we will discuss the common traits of this generation of job candidates and help you take stock of the specifics of your own situation. We'll also ask some difficult questions: are you making it harder for yourself to find a job than it needs to be? What's the real obstacle getting in the way of your success? Then we will walk job seekers through each step of our Candidate Illumination™ process. The objective of Candidate Illumination is to focus light on the job applicant, accentuating the key strengths that will separate a given candidate from the pack. More important, it's designed to make the candidate comfortable with the notion of standing out. The end benefit of

Candidate Illumination is confidence. Confidence is the first step to success in the real world and is the most important quality needed to effectively share a compelling personal brand story with a prospective employer. The Candidate Illumination process also dismisses many of the myths young people believe about the job search process.

Some say a superior education is its own reward and that coaching and counseling are simply means to that end. But shouldn't there be a support system in place to help bridge the gap between college and the working world? We think so. It's the reason we founded Hayden-Wilder and the reason we've written this book.

Every day, our offices are visited by some of the ever-growing number of bright, talented young people who graduated from college with all the hopes and dreams in the world, only to quickly find themselves stuck in a frustrating holding pattern. We take great pride in helping these young men and women, and we hope this book will give you the tools to find focus, get a job, and start a life.

1: THE ENTITLEMENT GENERATION

ENOUGH ABOUT YOU, LET'S TALK ABOUT ME

Ed Steinburg was feeling pretty good about himself. He'd just graduated with a degree in business from a large New England university. He was staying in his girlfriend's apartment, so he could live on the cheap and not feel pressured to pick the first job that came along.

He'd sent out more than a hundred resumes to companies he thought might be interested in his business background. It would be just a matter of time, he thought, before the offers started pouring in, and he'd had some nibbles already. A condiment manufacturer with a well-respected national brand wanted him to interview for a job in their marketing department. He turned them down. Marketing was interesting, but who cares about food? Then he was contacted by an international chain of high-end hotels. They expressed interest in his applying for their management training program. No dice. Too much travel, boring program, and pathetic salary.

He also had gone on a few informational interviews. At least they were good practice, and who knows? One of them could turn into a job. He thought the meetings went pretty well. The conversations with the interviewers were relaxed and informative, and he thought he'd made it pretty clear early on that he was not looking for a job that involved sitting in a cubicle or one that required dull and repetitive work, like filing or data entry. "You can train a monkey to do those tasks," he was fond of saying. After all, he had a business degree. He should be doing important work.

NO INTERVIEWER IS INTERESTED IN WHAT YOU DON'T WANT TO DO.

Three months later, Ed had broken up with his girlfriend, and was living temporarily at home. No job, no paycheck, no girlfriend, no opportunities. Last we heard, he was working in a local camera store, processing photos, waiting for some decent offers to pop up.

Was Ed just the victim of bad luck? (That's what he thinks.) Or had he engineered his own predicament? (That's what we think.)

On the face of things Ed had a lot going for him. He graduated from a good college with a major that, all his professors assured him, was a job offer

ARROGANCE IS CONFIDENCE'S EVIL TWIN.

slam-dunk. His grades were pretty good—not cum laude quality, but in the low threes. And at least, by his own admission, he interviewed well. How come he wasn't flooded with fabulous offers?

The simple answer? *Arrogance.* Ed made the fatal mistake of believing the high regard in which he held himself would instantly be shared by his prospective employers. Worse still, he passed this attitude along to his interviewers. After all, he reasoned, wasn't he just too good a candidate to pass up? At least Jiffy Foto thought so; Ed's currently working the 8:00 A.M. to 4:30 P.M. shift, with every other Saturday off.

It might be easy to think Ed's case is an isolated instance, that relatively few candidates approach job hunting with such a careless attitude. But unhappily, we see this theme played and replayed a thousand times, to one degree or another, among today's college graduates. It's not really arrogance in the truest sense of the word; it is more a combination of naïveté and entitlement. Naïveté because they know too little about how the business world works, entitlement because they believe they shouldn't have to learn.

Fairly or unfairly, today's crop of college students and recent graduates have been labeled the entitlement generation. And even if you think the accusation doesn't apply to you, you'll probably be given the label anyway as a member of your peer group. Just like boomers were labeled "hippies," and gen Xers were called "slackers."

Do we think that you are all a group of overprivileged and overindulged brats who have been born on third base and have expectations that exceed your abilities? Of course not. In fact, we are continually impressed by the brains, energy, and creativity of the students who pass through our doors. In fact, according to Jake Halpern, in a 2007 article in the *Boston Globe Magazine*, the narcissism of today's youth is an essential ingredient in the care and feeding of entrepreneurialism in America. And that's great for those of you who choose to build your own companies right from the start rather than work for someone else.

But we feel that many of your generation, like Ed in our case history, may begin the process of searching for a job weighed down by unreasonable expectations regarding their hireability, the salary levels they feel they deserve, how frequently they should be promoted, and the importance of the work they're willing to do. And these misunderstandings and others like them can cause problems.

So how does the working world view the average member of the entitlement generation? Their supporters see them as tech-savvy, civic-minded, racially tolerant, inquisitive, intellectually sophisticated, idealistic, family-oriented, and hardworking (as long as the work is interesting). Their detractors see quite another picture. In their eyes boomerangs (so called because they tend to bounce back home after graduation) are arrogant, spoiled, indecisive, dependant, insecure, disloyal, praise-hungry, materialistic, lazy, high-maintenance, coddled, and intolerant of paying their dues to get ahead. To entitlement-bashers, kids coming out of college approach prospective employers wanting it all. And they see no reason why they should have to wait for it. To an older manager who has risen through the ranks in the traditional way, this attitude is infuriating.

Where does this superiority complex come from? If you're looking to attach blame, there's plenty to go around. Blame it on the parents who tell their children every day that they deserve the best and then give it to them. Or the school system that restructures the grading scale by removing "F" as a failing grade and replacing it with "Deferred Achievement" so as not to damage the psyches of their substandard students. Or grade school teachers who bend over backward to instill self-esteem with games like The Magic Circle, in which one child every day wears an "I'm Great" button while all the other kids bury him or her with undeserved compliments. Point the finger at college professors who hand out A's for C− work to avoid confrontation with parents. Or the Internet and cell phone technology that provides instant access and gratification 24/7. Guess what? If boomers think today's kids are spoiled, boomers are the ones who made them that way.

And what do the members of the so-called entitlement generation think? Look up "The Entitlement Generation" on Google and read a few of their blogs. They think we (adults, boomers) are a bunch of bozos, technologically crippled, self-satisfied, married to convention, unimaginative, uncommunicative, overcompensated, money-hungry, status-obsessed, inflexible, talentless cretins.

There it is. Both sides of the argument out on the table. Neither of them particularly flattering. They think we're old-fashioned, we think they're arrogant. So what's new? Don't you think your mothers and fathers felt the same way about their parents? Bet they did. It's called the generation gap, and it's as old as time.

But forget, for a moment, who's right or who's wrong. It's a useless argument anyway.

From your point of view, isn't it excusable to think that if your parents have just shelled out more than $200,000 for a college diploma, or if you're leaving school reeling under the weight of crushing student loans, perhaps you deserve a preferential position at life's starting line? Guess again. Deserving has nothing to do with it. There are hundreds of thousands of recent graduates out there, and they all have the same claim. They spent just as much on their education, worked just as hard, and are carrying just as much debt. Unfortunately, in a world in which there are more good candidates than good jobs, all your college education buys you these days is the right to enter the race. Where you finish is your problem.

Every year, approximately 1.4 million students graduate from U.S. colleges. Assuming 25 percent of these apply for grad school, that leaves about 1.1 million who are seeking to enter the work force. Add to that, of course, any leftovers from the previous class who are still

LANDING A GREAT JOB MAKES GETTING INTO AN IVY LEAGUE COLLEGE LOOK EASY.

seeking work and you have what amounts to a very competitive hiring environment.

And even though organizations like NACE (National Association of Colleges and Employers) have comforted job applicants with statistics that showcase recent increases in entry-level hiring, remember two things. First, good companies will always hire the best and the brightest, so just because there are more available jobs, it doesn't mean companies have to lower their standards to fill them. Second, simply because overall entry-level hiring is up doesn't guarantee that there are more jobs available in your particular area of interest. Much of the increase predicted by NACE for 2007 came from robust demand from the accounting/consulting sector. Areas like marketing, financial services, and health care showed much more modest gains. The message: don't let statistics about hiring levels, however positive, lull you into thinking that you don't have to work hard or be aggressive in seeking and getting the job you want. Remember, at this point in your life you have no laurels to rest on. It'll take all your energy and brains to get the job you want.

Here's another way to look at it. Even the most sought-after Ivy League school will accept one candidate out of twenty into its freshman class. A major investment bank or large consulting firm may reject two hundred candidates to fill a single position. You do the math.

Let's assume for the moment that there's at least a grain of truth in the "entitlement" argument. Let's also accept that despite the loosening of the job market, competition has never been tougher, both because of the sheer number of candidates available and because of their heightened qualifications. Kids today don't just study Mandarin, for instance. They live in Nanjing for a year with a Chinese family and study economics, taught in Mandarin, at a local university.

What does all this mean to you as a recent grad? Here are some thoughts that might ease your transition into the lumpy landscape of the real world.

DON'T CONFUSE ARROGANCE WITH CONFIDENCE

Arrogance is the belief that you're better than everybody else. Confidence is belief in yourself. Big difference. By all means, take pride in your accomplishments. If you're not proud of what you've achieved, how can you expect an employer to be? But whether fair or not, today's interviewers and H.R. executives are highly sensitized to anything that smacks of entitlement. Why? Because they've been forewarned, by the press, by sociologists, and through their own experience, that kids come out of college with elevated images of their own value. And they're ready to pounce at the first sniff of self-importance or superiority. Yesterday's "cockiness" is today's "arrogance," and it can lose you a job in the blink of an eye.

DON'T GET A CASE OF THE "DON'TS"

Ask students to describe the type of job they're seeking, and some start with a list of all the things they *don't* want in a job. No getting coffee; no filing; no jobs staring at a computer screen; no cubicles; no travel; no boring, repetitive tasks; no public speaking; no spreadsheets; no nine-to-five work schedules.

Maybe we're old-fashioned, but almost every one of the jobs we've held over the years involves some or all of these "don'ts." But mixed in among all that drudgery were some pretty exciting and rewarding moments that made it all worthwhile. Every job, however glamorous it appears from the outside, has its boring moments. So be aware that when you rattle off your list of exclusions and qualifications, what you're really saying to your interviewer is "I'm too smart and well educated to waste my time doing menial stuff. You need to find important things for me to do."

Instead, try communicating your willingness to start at the bottom, to put in long hours when necessary. Acknowledge that you know most entry-level positions involve some tiresome work and that you have no problem doing it, as long as you're learning something in the process. And don't worry. You won't be doing it forever. If you're hired, it will be because some people in the organization think you show potential and can rise in the organization. No hiring manager ever got promoted by turning college-educated job candidates into file clerks. Sounds like common sense, doesn't it? You'd be amazed how many grads don't heed it.

BEWARE OF OVERSELLING

Inexperienced interviewees tend to fall in to two categories: those who underplay their strengths, and those who overplay them.

When we talk about overstating strengths, we are not talking about the rare applicant who purposely doctors a resume to impress an employer. It's the worst mistake a job seeker can make. Not only is it dishonest, it's also a crime, and if you get caught in the lie, which many do, it can ruin your life. Don't do it . . . *ever.*

In our definition of "overselling" we're talking about the unintentional inflation of your abilities, particularly in interviews. One of the most common interview questions is "Tell me about your strengths." This can be a tough one, because it calls on you to make value judgments about your abilities. Most young people are uncomfortable doing it. On the one hand, you don't want to be overly modest and risk downplaying your assets. On the other, you don't want to come off as boastful. So how do you play it? Some candidates, when asked about their strengths, say things like "Well, I'm a great writer, and as you can see from my resume, I have really good experience." Or, "I think I have strong leadership skills and am a very creative person." We hear this every day. We know they're only trying to draw attention to their strengths, but there are better ways to communicate the message without seeming self-centered or boastful.

There are a few basic rules about selling yourself. First, when it comes to experience, you basically don't have any. That's why you're an entry-level candidate. Companies assume you have a lot to learn. They also know that even though they'll be paying you from day one, you may not be a particularly useful or productive employee for some time. The real value of internships or summer jobs to an employer is that you'll have been exposed to an industry or skill and found it sufficiently interesting to pursue it.

For instance, if you want to pursue a career in communications and have interned at an advertising agency, what makes you of interest to an employer is not your experience. It's that you've seen how agencies work firsthand, liked what you saw, and have come to the interview motivated and with your eyes wide open. So don't tell your interviewer you have great experience. Tell him how much working at an agency has taught you about the business and how passionate you are about being part of it. It's a much sexier answer.

Second, avoid giving yourself qualities that are best bestowed by others, such as leadership, work ethic, or creativity. You can be a leader only if others follow you, and you're only seen as a hard worker when someone—hopefully a superior—says so. Want to communicate your work ethic? Cite by example. If your boss gives you an unexpected raise because of the long hours you've put in at a summer job, tell that story in describing your work experience. Your interviewer will get the message that you're a hard worker. If you want to showcase your creativity, tell a story about how you solved a problem by thinking "outside the box." It's a much more credible demonstration of your creative thinking, and it's the perfect balance of humility and confidence.

One more thing. Please, if you say you write well, make sure you do. Nothing is quite so embarrassing as a poorly written resume or cover letter created by a "good writer." If you have to talk about your writing skills, it's much better to say, "I'm told I am a good writer by my professors." At least somebody else is saying it. But beware: the minute you bring up your writing, you will be inviting closer examination of it. That's why we usually advise our clients to avoid citing this as a strength.

Certain jobs, however—public relations, journalism, editorial services—demand strong writing skills. These usually require you to provide writing samples from your coursework, previous jobs, etc. It's important to have them available. It will save time, and you'll appear well prepared. If the writing is good, it will speak for itself.

THE LOYALTY ISSUE: USE IT TO YOUR ADVANTAGE

Companies today are faced with a serious problem. In the next ten years, the boomer generation will become eligible for retirement. That means upwards of 50 percent of the corporate employees, from upper management to hourly wage earners, will be leaving the workforce.

So regardless of how employers feel about the high-maintenance entitlement generation, their survival depends on bringing young, new faces into their companies. That's why major employers are rethinking their recruiting and management strategies to woo and retain entry-level candidates.

But it is also true that millennials get a rap for being fickle and disloyal employees. It's the "I'll take this job until a better one comes along" syndrome.

No one disputes that corporate business has a certain degree of infidelity coming to them. Downsizing, layoffs, rightsizing, pension fund defaults, health-care coverage reductions, and outsourcing all contribute to the employee philosophy of "I have to take care of myself, because I know my company won't." The result is that many young employees can have as many as four or five jobs in a seven-year span and this scares the crap out of a lot of corporations. Not only are their long-term employees retiring, but also their replacement hires don't stay long enough to pay back the investment made to train them. And this costs American companies billions each year.

What does this mean to you as an interviewee? First, any signal you can send to a potential employer that suggests, however subtly, you may have long-term ambitions within the company will fall on very receptive ears. Don't worry: you're not trapping yourself into a life of servitude. You are simply saying that if everything works out, you can envision a lasting relationship, and that's music to an employer's ears.

The key word is "subtly." Obviously, the full-frontal approach won't work. "If you hire me I promise not to leave for at least five years." You'd sound foolish saying it. But other methods can convey the sentiment in a much more credible way.

> **YOU CAN CHANGE THE COMPANY AFTER YOU'RE HIRED.**

Here's an example. Almost every interview ends with, "Do you have any questions for me?" What if you asked, "If I were lucky enough to be hired, where do you think I might be in three years?"

Why is this a smart question? Because it communicates some very positive attributes about you to the interviewer. First, it says you're ambitious and want to move up through the organization. That's important. Don't forget, a hiring manager's job isn't just to hire competent people, it's to hire promotable people. Second, by asking about your role in the company's future, you are quietly suggesting that you see yourself as a long-term (read "loyal") employee. It's a great way to end an interview, and a terrific way to set yourself apart from the nondescript "job seeker."

One last thought. Maybe your generation does have a sense of its own entitlement. Maybe it doesn't. What's important to understand is that a job interview is the wrong place to tell a prospective employer what you think you deserve. Nobody ever lost out on a job by showing a little respect for the interviewer or by communicating a willingness to start at the bottom. You can change the company once you're hired. Until then a little humility goes a long way.

2: HELICOPTER PARENTS

THE CASE
AGAINST
PARENTAL
AIR COVER

Your mother regularly calls you at 7:00 A.M. to remind you not to be late to your Women's Studies class. Your father gently suggests he should accompany you on your next interview to help with any salary negotiations and other "business issues." You come home from class and find your mother in your dorm room cleaning out your closets. "I threw out those horrible ripped jeans of yours. They were absolutely filthy. You don't mind, do you?" And, of course, the most humiliating of all, "Professor O'Connell, I really don't understand why you only saw fit to give my daughter a B+ on her sociology midterm. She's never gotten less than an A–." Does any of this sound familiar?

Have these examples been exaggerated for purposes of demonstration? Absolutely not. Parental participation in every aspect of a child's life is so commonplace that "helicoptering" is a widely recognized term to describe the hovering parental presence. At minimum, helicopering is nothing more than an occasional annoyance, part of the sometimes arduous process of learning to strike out on your own and your parents learning how to let you. "I'm twenty-one years old, Mom; I really think I'm capable of buying my own underwear." Or, "Dad, I'm sure your friend has a beautiful daughter, but please stop trying to fix me up." At worst, the most intrusive helicoptering parents thrust themselves into the center of every major academic and social decision or controversy you face. These parents are so prevalent in their child's life they even have a special name: *blackhawks*. I'm sure you can guess why.

Do you think there's a distinction between a mother who regularly cleans her son's room, and a father who uses Facebook to do background checks on his daughter's new roommate, then petitions the college for a change because he doesn't like what he finds out? We sure do. The former may come from an understandable and forgivable desire for a parent to hold on a little longer to a child on the verge of becoming an adult. You'll do the same when your children grow up.

The latter, however selfless the parental motive, is an abridgment of every child's right to weigh choices, make their own decisions, and ultimately to live with the consequences of those decisions. The process is called growing up. It's one of the most important reasons you went to college in the first place, and it's one of the greatest gifts a college experience can impart. Be on your guard for those intrusive parents who, by thrusting themselves into the center of their child's college experience, prevent them from learning the basic skills needed to embark on a productive and rewarding adult life.

ARE YOU BEING HELICOPTERED?

Helicoptering parents can start as early as day care; become most intense up to and during college; and, as many hiring managers and human resource executives can tell you, may persist well into the early working years.

In their role as protectors, helicoptering parents see no problem in helping with homework, finding tutors to ensure better grades, or using personal trainers to guarantee stellar performance on the soccer field or hockey rink. In fact, they see it as their solemn duty. Add to that, ballet, flute lessons, choir practice to develop fledgling artistic muses, and mandatory community service projects to ensure understanding the importance of knowing how to share one's good fortune with those less fortunate. Pick some typical, overachieving sixth graders you know and ask about their daily schedules. You'll find they're busier than a White House press secretary—and they're only eleven years old!

> IN THEIR ROLE AS PROTECTORS, HELICOPTER PARENTS SEE NO PROBLEM DOING ALMOST EVERYTHING FOR YOU.

We have no objection to keeping busy. It's a great antidote to killing time watching music videos or playing video games. But ask a lot of these hyperprogrammed kids why they're so busy and they'll tell you to talk to their parents, because "they signed me up."

Controlling parents stake their claim early in their children's lives. It's not uncommon for highly competitive and overeager mothers and fathers to use professional consultants to ensure their children's acceptance into the "right" day care centers, the best nursery schools, or the most-sought-after summer camps.

And the pressure continues unabated through high school, reaching its peak during the college application process. If you want to see helicopter parents in all their finery, watch the dance to get their children into the most prestigious colleges. Start with tutors to improve course grades, then throw in an SAT coach to raise test scores. Add to that counselors, some charging up to $20,000, to help families navigate the complex college selection process. For dessert, throw in a creative adviser so that each essay is Pulitzer Prize–caliber. It's not unusual for some families to invest as much as $50,000 grooming their child for the college admission process, only to earn the right to pay an additional $40,000 with the first tuition check.

> **IT'S NOT UNUSUAL FOR SOME PARENTS TO INVEST $50,000 TO GROOM THEIR CHILDREN FOR THE COLLEGE ADMISSION PROCESS.**

Why should some parents care so deeply about what once was the exclusive domain of the student? Is it just separation anxiety? Is it the pain of letting go after so many years invested in their child's development? Maybe it's a natural extension of the new role of twenty-first-century parents as supporters and nurturers? Or, to take the more cynical view, it could be that some mothers and fathers view the quality of the child's college or university as the definitive acknowledgment of their superiority as parents. Good college, good parent. Bad college, bad parent. It's a baby boomer thing.

NOT ALL HELICOPTERS ARE ALIKE

In our experience, helicopter parents tend to fall into two groups. The first, and by far the most benign, are the "clingers." In our experience, they tend to be moms. (Fathers by and large reserve their interference for larger issues.) We meet many mothers who describe their child as "my best friend." These mothers may decorate dorm rooms and provide ongoing maid service. "Poor Sarah, she never has a minute to clean her own room." They religiously attend college orientation classes, sometimes with-

> **HELICOPTERS MAY EXPECT TO TALK TO YOU ON THE PHONE SIX TIMES A DAY OR MORE.**

out their child, and in some cases have been known to accompany their children to the first few days of class. These are parents who want to participate in every aspect of their child's development. To them, growing up is a team effort, and they insist on being in on every play.

Where once parents might have considered themselves fortunate to hear from their college student every week or so, the clinger phones or is phoned as many as half a dozen times a day. The dorm pay phone, with its long line of waiting callers, has been replaced by the ubiquitous cell phone. And kids pay dearly for the convenience.

Particularly in the freshman and sophomore years, parents help with course schedules, research classes, and in some cases even interview faculty members, all with an eye to making the transition from high school to college as low stress as possible. And yes, they have even been known to attend dorm mixers and intervene in roommate meltdowns. They check student e-mails, balance checking accounts, send rolls of quarters for laundry, surf Facebook to keep tabs on their kids and their friends, proofread term papers, and perform a thousand other services in their ongoing effort to "stay involved."

Remember your first few days of freshman orientation? Some parents couldn't wait to unload the car, kiss the kid good-bye, and be back on the road before the ink was dry on the tuition check. Others set up a base of operations in a local hotel, attended all the freshman receptions, took the roommates to dinner every night, scoped out the local malls, and shopped every bank in town for the best deals on checking and saving accounts. The college had to practically throw these parents out to get them to leave.

> **A "MY CHILD IS AN HONOR STUDENT" BUMPER STICKER IS THE HELICOPTER PARENT'S BADGE OF HONOR.**

In our view and certainly in the eyes of employers and colleges, the meddling and interference of these blackhawks crosses the line. They view their children as badges of their own accomplishment and success. Show us a bumper sticker that says "My child is an honor student," or an SUV plastered with prep school and Ivy League college decals, and we'll show you a potential exploiter in the making. If the clinger's motive is to give a child the best possible opportunity to succeed, the blackhawk seeks bragging rights. They are classic "Type A's"—competitive, controlling, and critical. Blackhawks are convinced they know what's best for their child, and have a detailed master plan that will, if followed, guarantee success. A "winner" child is by definition born of "winner" parents. It's classic blackhawk reasoning.

From time to time we get calls from blackhawk parents. The conversation often goes like this: "Our daughter just graduated from UCLA. We didn't want her wasting her college education on dead-end courses like psychology or philosophy, so we insisted she major in finance. After all, that's where the big money is. Who ever heard of a philosopher making a million dollars? Now she's out of school and telling us she doesn't want anything to do with banking. We give up. Maybe you can knock some sense into her head; she won't listen to us anymore."

Happily, blackhawk parents of this description are exceptions. But as any college dean or administrator can tell you, blackhawks are loudly steering their children into unwished-for career paths, doctoring resumes, and battling with college faculty and corporate human resource managers to push their kids to the front of the line.

MOMMY, WHERE DO HELICOPTERS COME FROM?

It might seem to many that helicoptering is a phenomenon confined to upper-middle-class America. After all, you must be rich to afford all the extra tutors, soccer camps, and college counselors that go with building the perfect kid. But in one of the first formal studies focused exclusively on the helicopter phenomenon, University of Texas at Austin data found that hovering, to one degree or another, appears to permeate all socioeconomic, racial, and ethnic communities. Moreover, it seems to be fairly widespread. According to college administrators and faculty of the surveyed institutions, 60 to 70 percent of parents exhibit some symptoms of the disease.

BOOMERS HAVE RAISED HELICOPTER PARENTING TO AN ART FORM.

So what is it about this parent generation that makes them so uniquely inclined to provide ongoing ground support and air cover for their children?

The point here is that while most experts agree that helicoptering is a growing national issue, no one really knows how widespread it is, nor exactly when the gentle parental guidance and support morphs into full-blown interference. However, it's a safe bet that parents are least likely to diagnose themselves accurately. Have you ever heard a mother or a father proudly announce that they're card-carrying helicopters? Not likely. Also, according to the study, many helicoptered kids don't seem to view parental interference with school faculty as embarrassing behavior. It seems that the definition of "humiliation" is more elastic than in previous generations.

What everyone seems to agree on is that helicoptering is a relatively recent term, having worked its way into the American vocabulary at about the time millennials began to enter college. And while boomers may not have invented the concept of parental interference, they are credited with raising its practice to an art form.

To those who make a living studying such matters, the largest share of blame is given to the cell phone. It's been aptly called the longest umbilical cord in the world. It's commonplace for elementary school children to carry a mobile phone with them everywhere. And

> **A CELL PHONE IS THE WORLD'S LONGEST UMBILICAL CORD.**

every parent whose kid is burning up a thousand minutes a month downloading ring tones or texting their friends will tell you that it's all about safety. It makes them feel better to know their child is always in reach.

While it's hard not to be sympathetic to the parent who wants to protect a son or a daughter in an increasingly dangerous world, we have yet to meet a child of any age who didn't view 24/7 accessibility as a mixed blessing. If your parents *can* reach you at any time, don't be surprised if they do.

So the habit starts early. Mothers call their children three or four times a day to check in. They arrange school pickups, carpooling to school and soccer. Cell phones are a godsend in straightening out fouled-up rendezvous or changes of venue. And guess what? By the time you're a senior in high school, have a driver's license, and an otherwise remarkable degree of independence, you still are tethered to your parents by phone. Did you really think your mother or father would stop calling just because you don't need them quite as much as you used to? Or because you've gone away to college? With a cell phone, there's no such thing as "out of sight, out of mind."

Another helicoptering reason, often cited by parents, is that college has become staggeringly expensive, even for reasonably affluent families. With tuitions at some private colleges approaching the $50,000-a-year mark, many families feel you'd have to be an idiot not to want to protect your investment. If a child, because of lack of guidance or self-discipline, gets thrown out at the beginning of a semester, kiss the $20,000 tuition payment good-bye.

There are other contributing factors. Some feel that the role of a college education has been redefined, particularly in the U.S. In earlier generations, college was considered the end of the road, a debarkation point for adult life. After college you got married, got a job, raised a family. Now the importance of college as a predictor of future success has been downgraded. It's still important, but viewed more as a fundamental extension of high school than as the ultimate educational experience.

And, of course, a large part of the helicopter mantra is generational. Boomers are protective. Remember the '90s bumper sticker, "Caution: Baby on Board"? Well, you are still that baby, only now you have a big sign on your back that reads "Quiet: College Student at Work."

Boomers are also intensely competitive. It's not enough that their children succeed. They are driven to be the first and the best. Do you think that your four years of soccer camp were all about having fun, getting exercise, and making new friends? Dream on. It was about winning, being a star, standing apart from your classmates. Ditto the college you get into and the first job you land after graduation. Is it any wonder that your parents seem so invested in your young life?

HELICOPTER PARENTS AREN'T HELPING YOU

Maybe we are being a little tough on these helicopters. After all, their motives are, for the most part, well intentioned. Their children have occupied a huge part of both of their lives. And now quite suddenly these same children all but evaporate, to live in a college community, often thousands of miles away, distant, and unfamiliar. Is it any wonder some parents look on their child's departure for college with a profound sense of dread? It's natural for some parents to want to soften the blow of this separation by trying to stay involved. They're just maintaining contact. "Dear, we don't mean to interfere, we're just trying to help."

HELICOPTER PARENTS THINK THEY'RE DOING WHAT'S BEST FOR YOU. THEY'RE NOT.

> **KEEP IN MIND THAT HELICOPTERS' MOTIVES ARE USUALLY WELL INTENTIONED.**

But here's the problem. College is *not* an extension of high school. It's a completely new and sometimes daunting experience. On the one hand, you enjoy more freedom than you ever thought possible. No one telling you when to go to bed, when to get up. Don't clean your room, no one cares. If you cut a class, you won't end up in the principal's office. You can even hit a concert the night before your math final without being grounded for the rest of your natural life. That's the good news.

The bad news? With all that freedom comes an equal measure of responsibility. In the college's eyes, you're not a kid anymore. You're old enough to behave like an adult. And adulthood means learning how to make decisions and accepting your mistakes. It's one of the most important lessons college has to teach and it's one of the main reasons you went to college in the first place.

Now let's suppose you have parents who decide they're going to participate in the decision-making process. They work out your class schedule, help you research a term paper. They choose your major and a thousand other things that make college life a little easier and less stressful. Yes, it's true, you'll probably avoid making some mistakes, but you won't be the captain of your life. You'll share the helm with your parents.

Worse still, you'll likely lose confidence in your own decision-making ability. It's why so many of the so-called millennials are accused of having difficulty making decisions and why they are criticized for needing continual affirmation and support.

In our work, we see so many clients, recently graduated from college, and impeccably educated, who are so afraid of making mistakes that they can't make even the simplest choices. "Can you look over my thank-you note and let me know if it's okay before I send it?" Or, "Should I sign my letter 'Sincerely' or 'Best regards'?" And, of course, our personal favorite: "The guy never called me back. Do you think it would help if my father gave him a call?"

Pick up virtually any of the hundreds of articles written about millennials or boomerangs. Almost every story talks about how newly minted employees have an insatiable thirst for support and reassurance. Today the former practice of semiannual performance reviews for lower-level executives has been replaced with the notion of continual employee/manager dialogue. Corporate executives are required, in many companies, to attend seminars to more effectively communicate with their junior employees. Even basic daily tasks—writing a memo, working on a project, completing an assignment—demand instant feedback. It's no wonder today's young adults are often labeled as high maintenance by their coworkers.

> **MILLENNIALS HAVE AN INSATIABLE THIRST FOR REASSURANCE.**

So why is the most privileged, best-educated, most well-traveled, globally aware, and culturally sophisticated generation in history so lacking in self-confidence? Perhaps because parents, mentors, coaches, advisers, and counselors have effectively insolated a large portion of today's generation of young adults from the sometimes painful lessons associated with growing up. Remember, as comforting as it may be to accept support from your mother or father, no parent is doing you a favor by repaving the road to your adulthood. At some point they're not going to be around to hold your hand. Then who are you going to ask?

HELICOPTER PARENTS BREED HELICOPTER KIDS

When you read some of the horror stories about parental interference, don't you ask yourself why their children don't rebel? After all, having your father get into an argument with your history professor over your exam grade has to rank right up there on the embarrassment barometer. Why stand for it?

Some don't. A number of hovered-over kids push back. They find imaginative ways of staying out of the glare of the parental spotlight. Cell phones get turned off, too-frequent calls go unreturned, lingering parents are gently nudged off campus. After a while, even the most thick-skinned mother or father gets the hint and fades into the background.

But what about the others? Is every outrageous act of parental interference committed over the strident objections of the child? We don't think so. In our experience as counselors and hiring managers, we've run across any number of intrusive parents. But what's interesting is that a large number of their kids accept and even welcome this level of intrusion. It's impossible to visualize a parent accompanying a job applicant on an interview if the candidate is dead set against it.

> "MOM, THEY'RE MY MISTAKES. I CAN MAKE THEM ON MY OWN."

According to an online survey conducted by Experience, Inc., a provider of career services to students and grads, approximately 25 percent of polled college students described their parents as overly involved, meaning to the point of annoyance or embarrassment. What is astonishing, however, is that almost 40 percent of students say their parents have had some interaction with college advisers and almost a third (31 percent) freely admit that their parents have called professors to argue about grades. If that's not embarrassing, what is?

Why does this happen? Lots of reasons. First, most children are brought up to trust their parents. If your father says it's a good idea that he accompany you to an interview, he ought to know. He's your dad. He has more work experience than you do. Your natural instinct is to abdicate to his wishes.

Another reason. If your parents have been calling the shots since you were a child, micromanaging your life from grade school through college, it's hard to suddenly dig your heels in when it comes to looking for a job. You've been preconditioned to expect, maybe even welcome, parental meddling. You're so used to it, it doesn't seem out of the ordinary. According to the Experience, Inc., study, a parent has to interfere big time to qualify as annoying.

We acknowledge that most helicopter parents honestly believe they're helping their kids.

After all, isn't that what being a good parent is all about? But the sad truth is that, however well intentioned, they're actually holding their children back, making it much more difficult for them to develop the skills they'll need to succeed in the real world.

If you feel your parents are playing too large a part in your life, gently remind them (you'll probably have to do it more than once) that you're an adult now and you need to make your own decisions. You'll make a mistake or two along the way. Big deal.

Everybody does. Make them, learn from them, and move on. It's the adult thing to do.

DO YOU TEST HP-POSITIVE?

Take this quiz to measure your level of helicopter parenting (HP).

My parents call me:
1. once per week or less (+5).
2. at least twice per week (0).
3. every day (-10).
4. don't know; I smashed my phone (+10).

I call them:
1. once per week or less (+5).
2. at least twice per week (0).
3. every day (-10).
4. they disconnected their phone (-10).

My parents talk to my professors:
1. over my dead body (+10).
2. occasionally (0).
3. regularly (-5).
4. they're on their speed dial (-10).

My parents help me choose my:
1. courses (0).
2. major (-5).
3. room decor (-10).
4. boy-/girlfriend (-100).

My parents accompany me:
1. to a class (0).
2. to a job fair (-5).
3. to an interview (-20).
4. on a date (seek professional help).

After graduation my parents want me to move home:
1. no way (+10).
2. maybe (+5).
3. they can't wait (-10).
4. they are building me my own apartment over the garage (-20).

When I get a job my parents want me to:
1. be happy (+20).
2. be self-supporting (+10).
3. become rich (0).
4. support them (-100).

I make all the major decisions about my life:
1. always (+20).
2. sometimes (+10).
3. occasionally (-5).
4. I don't know; call my mom (-50).

Have your parents ever helped you write a paper?
1. never (+20).
2. once (0).
3. sometimes (-10).
4. not since my dad got a C– on one of my sociology papers (-50).

How to calculate your score

+30 or higher:	Congratulations. You're a practicing adult.
+10 to +30:	You're doing great. Your parents are practically paper trained.
+10 to −5:	Keep it up. You have your parents under control.
−5 to −50:	Uh oh. Watch the rotor blast.
−50 or less:	Dial 911.

3: MANAGING YOUR PARENTS

DAAAD. . . IT DOESN'T WORK THAT WAY ANYMORE

How frightening. You've graduated from college. You have a degree in hand that is worth, in many cases, upwards of $200,000. You're leaving all your college friends behind. You're moving back home. You don't have a job. And the only people who are giving you job-hunting advice are your parents. It's no wonder this is the scariest transition of your life.

You're not alone. Over the years, both at Hayden-Wilder and in earlier iterations of our careers, we've seen countless candidates whose sole source of advice and counsel is their parents. The net result: wrong information, false starts, frustration, and loss of confidence.

It's pretty easy to understand the issue from your parent's point of view. They've paid hundreds of thousands of dollars over the course of your life to raise you in the best way they could possibly afford. Your parents have been with you, at your side, as an active participant or coach from your first day of pre-school, to kindergarten and elementary school, through the traumatic middle school years, at your high school graduation, on your first day of college, and upon receipt of your graduation diploma. And, then you jump into a world

beyond your parent's immediate control. There is no easily obtained, charted map that parents can give children for the post-college, real-world phase of their lives. Your parents see you swinging in the wind, and they want to be your safety net. They want to see the years of education they've provided yield the best results possible for you.

As parents tell us over and over, they want to see their children succeed … but it's so hard to let go. Real separation anxiety can set in. Many parents we've interviewed freely admit they are not qualified to guide their child in a chosen career path, nor are they in a position to help their unfocused liberal arts graduate choose a career direction. But, parents being parents, they somehow or another get themselves involved; either by worrying, nagging, or pushing.

We know your parents want to do the right thing. They've made a huge financial and emotional investment in your education, and they want everything to turn out well for you. They are as nervous as you are, which is why tensions are running high and every conversation seems to revolve around launching your career.

Some parents are better than others when it comes to the challenges and decisions their children face in determining a career path. We've met parents who are extremely nonchalant, encouraging their child to take a year off to travel or work at a menial job to "clear their head and take a break" after the stress of college. Or those who endorse their child's decision to take six months to waitress and ski in Colorado (even if six months morphs into two years). In some ways these parents are procrastinating as much as their children are. We've also met some who have been micromanaging their child's career direction since the sixth grade. What's important for you to realize is that it doesn't matter whether your parents fall into the first or the second category; they will be involved in your career decisions in one way or another. And even if your parents claim they are leaving you on your own, you know full well you will probably wonder at some point if they will approve of the direction you've chosen.

Parents *can* play a valuable role in the job search process. As the candidate, you will need to manage their role and help everyone in the family realize the dynamics of today's job search process. After all, the entry-level requirements of today's workplace are vastly different from those of the 1970s and '80s, when your parents were launching their careers.

CONNECTIVITY BREEDS COMPETITION

E-mail, cell phones, BlackBerries, PDAs, iPhones, text messaging, Bluetooth technology, and so much more have helped create both a generation and a workforce of highly connected people who work and communicate at warp speed. The job search process has been enormously affected by connectivity—the Web is the preeminent research vehicle, first-round interviews are often conducted by cell phone, e-mail leaves no "float" time for delayed thank-you notes, and responses to questions are routinely sent via BlackBerries while hiring managers are in transit to and from the office.

There are very few "unpublicized" job opportunities anymore, as even those job postings that have traditionally been posted in-house at companies are frequently electronically communicated by company employees to outside friends. In a connected world, opportunities for employment can be communicated to thousands of people in minutes.

Importantly, for all jobs, connectivity, agility, multitasking skills, and computer literacy in all basic office software (including Excel!) are prerequisites for entry-level candidates. Compare this skill set with the big question your mother may have been asked when she was looking for her first job: "How many words a minute can you type?"

UNLESS YOU INTEND TO COMMIT CANDIDATE SUICIDE, CLEAN UP YOUR FACEBOOK PROFILE.

The vast majority of today's workforce doesn't benefit from having an assistant helping them in their daily routine. And those daily routines are getting longer and longer. The average entry-level employee works more than fifty hours a week, compared to the forty-hour workweek enjoyed just two decades ago.

Of course, the downside to connectivity is that everyone knows everyone else's business. The majority of employers today have access to Facebook, MySpace, and other social networking sites. They are actively checking these sites to see what prospective candidates are sharing online. If the human resources department and the direct hiring manager aren't checking, it's a sure bet that many of the employees you met while you were interviewing are.

Case in Point Our client **Tommy Han** committed candidate suicide when he interviewed for a position and neglected to clean up his Facebook profile. Unfortunately, there was some weird and ugly information to be found, and it was immediately shown to the hiring manager. Tommy found out later, from a friend within the company, that his Facebook entry had nixed his chances of landing the job he wanted.

Our advice: either completely sanitize your profiles, or get rid of them entirely. It will save you a lot of embarrassment in the long run.

PARENTS ARE A KEY RESOURCE; USE THEM WISELY

How can you possibly begin the search process and still keep your parents at bay? The answer is quite simple: *take control.* This is a point we state over and over with our clients, and it is perhaps the most important step you can take at this very moment. We talk about taking control throughout this book. You are at a time in your life when *you* deserve to be in control instead of a friend, teacher, parent, or potential employer. Our program, called Candidate Illumination, is all about putting the spotlight on you, and using every resource you have to control the outcome and secure the job you want.

> **MANAGE YOUR PARENTS; DON'T WAIT FOR THEM TO MANAGE YOU.**

Experience tells us that the less information you share with your parents, the more skeptical they will become. We also know that the more information you share with your parents, the more involved (to the drive-you-insane level) they will become in your search. So the challenge is to strike the right balance between oversharing information and not sharing information at all.

Let your parents know they can positively and constructively support your search in a variety of ways:

1. **Parents may advise, but never write, the candidate's resume.** We've seen too many cases of parents writing resumes they think are great, but unfortunately, the candidate can't explain what's on the resume and doesn't know what half of it means.

We've also seen cases where parents can catch and fix a resume mistake—in work chronology, or the legal name of a former employer, for example—which averts providing misinformation to potential employers and eliminates embarrassing questions for the candidate.

IF YOUR PARENTS WANT TO WRITE YOUR RESUME, JUST SAY NO!

2. **Parents should encourage the candidate to spread his or her wings, and share in exploring a variety of career options.** Often parents, in thinking they are doing the best for their child, insist on pursuing a field that is of little or no interest to the child. The parent may be pointing in the direction of perceived future monetary success and opportunity for advancement when the child is looking for a more intellectual or creative outlet. Pushing a child into a singular field can often backfire, either in a flat-out rejection of the suggestion, or by sidetracking an otherwise productive search. We've all met a candidate who, later in life, makes a difficult career change and blames his parents for "pushing him in the wrong direction" after college.

3. **If parents have children who want to follow in the same career path as their parents, it's incumbent on the parent to share the good, bad, and ugly about the chosen career.** Honesty, and identifying potential potholes, are of utmost value to the candidate. And every profession has its own specific nuances and language; parents can be great decoders of this information. Most importantly, parents of children entering a similar career can create a comfort zone between their child and the chosen career path.

4. **Open communication between parents and children is critical.** Candidates need to show parents they have a search plan that includes benchmarks for success and opportunities for parents to help in the networking process. In so doing, the candidate, not

the parent, is controlling the process, while the parent is working to make the effort as fruitful as possible.

5. **Parents should never accompany candidates on job interviews or even at informational meetings.** Nor should parents ever negotiate salary or benefits on behalf of their children. Likewise, don't share corporate "parent information packs" with your parents unless you are truly interested in joining the company providing the information.

Case in Point ➤ **Sanford Pershing,** a client of Hayden-Wilder, is an Ivy League university graduate with a degree in government and a minor in economics. Sanford had completed studies abroad at the London School of Economics and had interned as an assistant to the U.S. congressman from his district. He had also worked one summer as a research assistant for an investment bank, which had an office in his hometown. Sanford came to us wanting to pursue a career in commercial real estate. Sanford's father, knowing nothing about the commercial real estate business, was convinced Sanford was better suited to the investment banking business. That's where the problems began.

Sanford knew that even though his major was government, he didn't want to get into politics or public policy and was not interested in going directly to grad school to study diplomacy. He wanted to get out in the world, have a challenging career, and start making some money on his own. Logically, Sanford thought his studies in government helped him understand how states, cities, and municipalities ran, and his background in economics gave him a perspective on business and its impact on local economies. Sanford had a couple of classmates at college whose fathers were in commercial real estate. It sounded interesting, and toward the end of his senior year, Sanford found himself reading about the most recent real estate deals in the paper every day. He then started to read deeper and learn about incentive programs state governments were offering companies to build facilities and bring employees to specific locations.

Just prior to graduation, Sanford told his parents he had decided he wanted to get into commercial real estate. Sanford's mother, who told him she would be proud of him no matter what he did, thought commercial real estate sounded like a fine idea. Sanford's father, however, had a very different reaction.

Unbeknownst to Sanford, his father, who is a successful investment banker, had talked to several of his friends about his son who was soon to be graduating from college. Sanford's father had just assumed his son would go into investment banking (even though Sanford had not participated in on-campus investment banking interviews); after all, he'd be the perfect candidate and could easily begin meeting with many of his father's friends. What's more, Sanford's father had written his son's resume as a part of his upcoming graduation gift. What more did Sanford need?

Sanford followed his father's wishes and began meeting with his father's friends, both for informational interviews and for real jobs. Guess what? Little interest, no takers. Why? Because at every interview Sanford said "I'm *thinking* about going into investment banking" rather than "I'm really looking forward to a career in investment banking." The result: Sanford's father's contacts knew right away that Sanford was not passionate about the investment banking business, so they conducted courteous meetings and then never contacted Sanford again. Sanford's father seriously sidetracked what could have been a much more productive and fruitful job search experience.

After meeting with Hayden-Wilder, and following several candid conversations between Sanford and his father, we managed to get Sanford back on track with his focus on commercial real estate. And, interestingly enough, Sanford met a second time with several of the original contacts his father had suggested. Many of these investment banking professionals had commercial real estate connections they were more than happy to introduce to Sanford.

Sanford is now working at a major international real estate development firm. He finds that his background in economics has really helped him understand some of the financial complexities of the deals in which he is involved. What's more, Sanford's government studies paid off as he helps navigate the many hurdles his company faces as they promote building and developing mixed-use facilities in lower-income urban neighborhoods. Sanford loves his job, has been promoted twice, and his father is his biggest advocate.

The moral of Sanford's story is that he realized after his financial services search debacle that he, not his father, was in charge of his own destiny. So with a plan in hand, he *took control*. Sanford actively involved his father in a way that could be productive, and his father, in turn, felt as though he had been influential in the outcome of his son's search.

SO, WHAT DO I GET FOR MY $200,000?

When we started Hayden-Wilder, we talked to many different audiences about college career services and the value those departments provide. We met with a number of college career services counselors (both on and off campus), reviewed their materials, and assessed their service offerings. In conversations with lots of parents of college students and college students themselves, a totally different perspective of the value of career services began to emerge:

- If you talk with staff members of most college career services departments at universities and colleges across the country, they will tell you they do a good job working with students to get them ready to launch their careers and land their first jobs out of college.

- If you talk with parents of juniors in college, the majority will tell you they are relying on college career services to find their child a job during their senior year of college, so their child will be all set upon graduation.

- If you talk with these same parents during the second semester of their child's senior year in college (assuming their pending graduate is one of the million-plus U.S. students who has not landed a job), these parents will tell you they are worried about the help their child is receiving from college career services.

- If you talk with students who are juniors or seniors in college, a significant number of them will tell you they received little or no help from college career services and think the department and its staff are a waste of time.

- If you talk with our clients at Hayden-Wilder, many will say college career services did not give them the type of help they needed, or that career services gave them bad advice. Or worse, that the reputation of career services among students was so bad that they avoided the department entirely.

> **UTILIZE CAREER SERVICES AS A RESOURCE,
> NOT A PLACEMENT SERVICE.**

WHAT IS COLLEGE CAREER SERVICES?

College career services is exactly what its name describes: a service organization. It is not a placement agency, nor is it charged with guaranteeing every graduate a job. Unfortunately, as the price of tuition and of room and board continues to increase, the natural assumption is that all college departments and services will improve in direct proportion to the price increase. What's more, when college and university admissions officers market their colleges' attributes to prospective freshmen, many refer to the great jobs and careers their alumni enjoy. Alas, the profound myth of career services as the great job placement office is perpetuated.

MOST CAREER SERVICES STAFFERS DON'T CARE IF YOU GET A JOB.

Every career services office is different. Some are very small; others are larger. Some offer extensive services; others are more of a drive-through experience. Some offer individual attention over time; others provide limited one-on-one interaction. Over the past few years we've met with many career services departments, and we are continually amazed by the tremendous differences among them.

For example, the career services office of one major city university with a huge alumni network will only see students for appointments of fifteen minutes at a time. This means, once initial pleasantries are exchanged, the student has about ten minutes of questions and answers, after which he must book time again, most likely in the following week. What can possibly be accomplished in this sort of atmosphere and time frame? No wonder many parents of graduates of this school are frustrated. What's more, this same university limits use of the career services office to one year after graduation, at which point graduates can no longer receive help.

On the flip side, when we met with career services at a very exclusive private women's college, we were pleased to see the office offer a more robust menu. This college also requires the companies interviewing students on campus to provide written feedback to each student interviewed. Feedback of this type is invaluable if it is channeled in the right direction and used as a basis for improvement in interviewing skills. That's when it's important for the college not to drop the ball.

Case in Point We worked with a senior, **Callie Stenapolis**, while she was attending an extremely prestigious college in New York City. Callie had signed up for a variety of on-campus interviews and felt as though she bombed time and again. Prior to meeting with us, she went to career services for help. After participating in a thirty-minute mock interview, Callie reported that the advice she received from career services was that she needed more confidence. Period. No further instruction on how to develop the required confidence. She was given a workbook to study and told to come back when she was ready to interview again. That's where, despite a strong reputation for helping students, this career services department committed a fatal error. They told a student what was wrong with her but offered no solution for future success. Talk about being left swinging in the wind!

Rather than just commenting on a lack of confidence, the career services department should have identified the areas in which Callie was weakest and helped her develop the requisite content and delivery skills. We all know it's difficult to project confidence when you don't believe in what you're saying. Or worse, it's hard to project confidence when you answer a question and know in your heart of hearts that you have no idea what you are talking about. We are not all born bullshitters, and every good interviewer can spot a bullshitter a mile away anyhow. Only when you are comfortable with the content of your answers can

BEWARE:
INTERVIEWERS
HAVE BUILT-IN
BULLSHIT DETECTORS.

you begin to develop confident delivery skills. (In chapters 13, 14, and 15 of this book, we share lots of information to help you develop confidence when interviewing.)

At a nationally respected business-focused university known for its high-tech teaching methods and entrepreneurial focus, the career services department offers videotaped interviews, which are conducted by computer. Students can then play back their interviews on their PCs. Unfortunately, that's as far as it goes. There is no formal critique process to help students improve their interview skills. We think this is an irresponsible high-tech "teaching tool," because it doesn't really teach. What's more, business majors who aspire to be entrepreneurs need great interviewing and presentation skills to raise the money they need to make their fledgling businesses succeed.

COMPETENT ADVISERS OR STUDENT PEERS?

We've also spent a significant amount of time analyzing the capabilities of individual career services staff members. The vast majority of career services staffers we have met, or those who have worked with our clients, are well-meaning but not truly capable of making a difference in a student's life.

Many career services staffers are grad students, biding time before they themselves have to enter the real world. Others are twenty- to thirty-year veterans of the career services department, with little to no real-world work experience. The veterans told us they are very connected because companies visit their campus. When we asked if they ever proactively visited corporations, the answer was generally no. These veterans also freely admitted they didn't really

> **MANY CAREER SERVICES STAFFERS ARE GRADUATE STUDENTS, BIDING TIME BEFORE THEY THEMSELVES HAVE TO ENTER THE REAL WORLD.**

have the ability to spend significant amounts of time with students. Several career services veterans told us they have their own ways of discouraging students from making multiple appointments with their career advisers. It's no wonder booklets, videos, and pamphlets are the mainstay tools of career services staffers. They don't have time to do anything more.

One of our clients, **Betsy Ruggles**, graduated from a large midwestern state university, with a degree in English. Betsy made several visits to career services and worked with one graduate student in particular, who truly wanted to help her with her resume. But rather than working to have her author her own resume, the graduate student in career services took it upon herself to rewrite Betsy's resume. In her zeal to make Betsy attractive to potential employees, the graduate student superinflated her work experience. Betsy's one-month internship at a local television station became a full-time assistant producer position. The work Betsy did helping raise money for AIDS awareness became much bigger than it actually was, and positioned her as the leader of the fund-raising effort. The graduate student created inflated titles for all of Betsy's summer jobs and internships, implying much more responsibility than she actually had. But the worst thing about this resume-writing exercise was that the graduate student convinced Betsy that her new resume was beyond reproach. She was told, "Everybody does this. We have to make your experience more compelling. You need better titles for your summer jobs."

And then the awful, awkward moment arrived. Betsy used the resume in an on-campus interview and was not able to explain the work she did in her overly exaggerated job descriptions. She found herself saying, "Well, actually, it was more like this . . ." Betsy couldn't live up to her resume. The graduate student working in career services did her a major disservice.

GETTING THE MOST OUT OF CAREER SERVICES

Career services offices are simply not strong enough to offer long-term, individualized counsel until the student finds a careerworthy job. No career services office in the country has the bandwidth, industry connections, or real-world expertise to offer students the type of hand-holding guidance to which they've become accustomed in all other aspects of their lives. And the majority of career services departments are measured by the college on the

> **USING CAREER SERVICES PROPERLY IS A KEY COMPONENT OF CONTROLLING YOUR JOB SEARCH PROCESS.**

number of students they "touch" (walk in, grab a brochure, have a fifteen-minute conversation, use the database) rather than the number of students they effectively guide into a terrific first job.

While all of this may sound harsh, it's important to recognize both the weaknesses and the strengths of career services and to examine how to get the most out of the department. Using career services properly is a key component of controlling your job search process.

We always suggest that our clients touch base with career services and schedule an appointment to discover what resources are available. By far the most important resource a career services department can offer is its alumni database and a list of the businesses their graduates are in. By accessing this database, you are establishing the basis for lots of significant networking and intelligence-gathering in the field you want to pursue. Many colleges have separate databases of alumni who are interested in talking to graduates and encourage graduates to arrange appointments to meet for informational interviews. Other schools simply list the alumni by city and/or industry. The rest is up to the graduate.

Career services is also the central organizer of on-campus visits by outside companies, recruiters, government organizations, and various programs, including Americorps and others like it. Go to the career fairs on campus. Check out the companies visiting to recruit graduates. Even if none of the jobs interests you, it's a great exercise in getting to know what's out there.

The key to all of this is to think of career services as an important tool in your arsenal, not as a placement service.

WHAT IF I DON'T HAVE A CLUE WHAT I WANT TO DO?

This is the most difficult question a college career services professional encounters, and it is the question they are least equipped to answer. This question is even more difficult to answer when the student is a liberal arts graduate. Most often, career services will try to connect a student's major area of study with a job that directly correlates with that area. Their advice: Accounting majors should become accountants. Biology majors should become biologists. English majors should work in the world of publishing. Government majors should become state or federal government employees. And so on and so on.

ADVICE FROM CAREER SERVICES CAN BE FLIPPANT AND CONFUSING.

But what about the grad who (1) doesn't feel comfortable or excited about following the predictable career path, or (2) has majored in a field like philosophy, sociology, women's studies, history, or comparative religions, where predictable paths are not so easily found? To address these needs, many career services professionals will resort to standardized testing to help steer the graduate in the right direction. But standardized tests are just that: they're standardized. These tests will give you a variety of options, oftentimes with multiple and conflicting directions. We've also seen tests that give our clients so many options it makes them more confused than they were in the first place.

Case in Point → Our client **John Simpson** was a double major in philosophy and history at a small liberal arts college in Connecticut. John had no idea what he wanted to do after graduation, but he did know he wanted to do something "rewarding." He went to career services for advice.

After a couple of frustrating meetings, John and his contact at career services decided John should take a series of standardized tests to determine potential career directions John could pursue. After taking the tests, the resulting feedback was more confusing than John

THE DOS AND DON'TS OF WORKING WITH CAREER SERVICES

Don't rely on or expect career services to find you a job.

Don't let career services write your resume or cover letter.

Don't take the recommendations of standardized tests to heart.

Don't wait to visit the career services office until the end of your senior year.

Don't let your parents call career services on your behalf; they won't get anywhere.

Do visit career services in the second semester of your junior year.

Do attend career fairs hosted by career services.

Do access the alumni database organized by career services; these are the people who are willing and able to help you.

Do push for as much information as you can get regarding scheduled on-campus interviewing sessions with outside companies.

Do post your resume and cover letter on the university/career services Web site, if such a service is available.

had ever imagined. His interests were apparently so broad he would be well suited to work in everything from the FBI to pharmaceutical sales. In what John believes was a move to placate him, his career services contact suggested John go to graduate school to study history, or spend a year teaching English to poverty-stricken children in Central America. Both opportunities would be "rewarding," and incidentally, provide no salary. John was flabbergasted at the suggestions and too frustrated to even laugh it off.

After working with us, he decided to focus on a career in development and fund-raising and landed a job working with a major national health organization. He has a "rewarding" job, uses the talents he honed in college, and loves every minute of it.

We believe it's really important to understand the motivations of our clients, beyond their academic studies. We also believe that some of the key skill sets found in liberal arts graduates are applicable to any number of fields, and we love working with clients who have studied languages, art, philosophy, anthropology, and all the various liberal arts disciplines. Interestingly, many of these students underestimate the power of a liberal arts education and the great flexibility it gives them in the work world. Many career services offices find liberal arts majors frustrating to work with, as a broad perspective and a creative approach to career selection are required to satisfy a liberal arts grad.

BIG COMPANIES ARE NOW SEEKING OUT LIBERAL ARTS GRADS.

About 75 percent of the liberal arts students we see don't know what they want to do after graduation. Or they are intrigued with a particular area but don't know much about it. These are students who went to career services to ask about careers in advertising, but no one could explain the structure of an advertising agency. Or these are English majors who want to write for a living yet actually make a decent wage. No one in career services told these English majors about the abundance of corporate writing opportunities, because no one in career services understands the discipline.

Knowing what to expect from career services is the name of the game. Students who go in expecting career services to land them a job will be in for a shock. Prepare to utilize them for what they can do for you—provide alumni contacts, set up job fairs—but arm yourself with the knowledge that you will be doing the heavy lifting.

5: MOVING BACK HOME

I'M AN ADULT, CAN I COME HOME NOW?

47% OF GRADUATING STUDENTS MOVE HOME AFTER COLLEGE.

There's no question about it: the world has become an outrageously expensive place to live in. Get a cup of coffee before class: you're out $3.50. Buy the textbook your psych professor says is mandatory for your criminal justice class, fork over $50.00. And then there's bottled water, more expensive by the gallon than gasoline.

Add to that the cost of dating, driving, food, clothing, cable, video games, sports tickets, parking, parking tickets, and the occasional beer, and it adds up to a fairly hefty monthly number. And don't forget you're still in college, where your room and board have often been paid for.

It's true that some students are totally subsidized by their parents. We've even heard of cases in which some students have received allowances of $50,000 a year or more. If you're one of those, feel free to skip this chapter. But it's also becoming common for a student to hold down one or more jobs to make ends meet. If you're not working yourself, it's a safe bet you know a number of others who do.

So, you reason, if I can't afford to support myself in college, where all my major expenses are taken care of, how in God's name can I hope to make it on my own after I graduate, particularly on the crappy salary that comes with an entry-level position? Your conclusion: I have no choice but to move home until I can make enough/save enough to move out. That's why, according to a 2006 MonsterTrak study, up to 47 percent of students surveyed said they planned to move home for some period of time after graduation. It's why they call your generation boomerangs.

It's all too tempting for members of the older generation to look on this migration homeward as a sign that young adults today are too indulged for their own good and parents are too permissive. And perhaps to some degree that's true. But, despite the "When I was your age" clucking from some of the boomer generation, as far as we're concerned, there's nothing innately wrong with returning home after graduation. The issue is one of motive. The question you have to ask yourself is, "Am I moving home because I need to, or am I doing it because it's easier, safer, and cheaper than trying to make it on my own?" Some food for thought.

A DOSE OF REALITY

One thing is certain. Living at home will bear no resemblance to the life you lived in college. First, even though you'll have your parents around, all your friends will have gone their separate ways. Your new community will consist of two people thirty or so years your senior who'll go to bed after *Dateline* and throw barbecues on weekends. The bad news: don't be surprised if you find living at home a little lonely. The better news: if you do it right, it'll only be temporary.

Also, have the courtesy to remember that even though you're saving money by living at home, your parents aren't. Having you there costs real money. We're not suggesting, as some authorities do, that you need to pay rent or significantly share in household expenses, but it might be thoughtful to keep your room clean enough so it doesn't lower property values and every once in a while run an errand or wash a dish or two. If you want to watch your mother faint dead away, try doing your own laundry.

HAVE AN EXIT STRATEGY

Ask most graduates why they move home and they'll say, "to save money." It's a perfectly legitimate reason. But it doesn't go far enough. We've talked to scores of graduates who are living at home and presumably putting money away each pay period. But very few of them can tell you what they're saving for. The answer always seems to be the same: "to get enough so I can get a place of my own." If you ask them what it'll take and how long, most don't know.

Do yourself a favor. Set some goals. "I'll live at home until I've saved $2,000 for my share of the rent on an apartment and some furniture" is a lot better than " I'll move out when I've saved some money." Why?

Because open-ended goals aren't really goals at all. Give yourself a target and you'll always know how far you've got to go and how long it will take you to get there. And remember that word "control"? You'll feel better controlling your own destiny, and your parents will thank you. Take our word for it.

AVOID THE EASY MONEY TRAP

One thing's for certain: if you don't have a job by the time you graduate, living at home is your only option. That is, unless your parents are willing or able to bankroll an apartment and living expenses while you look for employment. And while it sounds obvious that getting a job should be your first and most important priority, be careful not to fall into the trap of postponing meaningful job searching by working at dead-end jobs that may pay well but lead you nowhere.

Case in Point **Timothy Mariani** graduated from a small northwestern college with a degree in sociology. Unfortunately, he didn't start thinking about what he might want to do after college until very late in his final semester. The result: he had no job after graduation and no strategy for getting one. Tim was headed home.

His parents were only too delighted to have him back under their roof. They gave him his old room, fed him when he was around (which was almost never), washed his clothes, and even let him use their second car. All they asked was that he pay for his personal expenses.

Ultimately, Tim got a job working as a laborer for a medium-size construction company in Warwick, Rhode Island. The pay was great, $16.00 an hour, and while the work was tough, he was off at four in the afternoon and had money to burn. That was two years ago. Today he's still at home and still working in construction. The only thing that's changed is that now he's earning $18.50 an hour and has bought his own car.

Let's forget, for a second, that Tim's parents may be on the brink of insanity because their adult son has been sharing their home for the past two years. And forget that most parents would not consider a career in construction a reasonable return on their $200,000 educational investment. The greatest sin is that Tim has wasted two years that could have and should have been used to begin his search for a job related to his education. In short, his classmates have left him in the dust. Worse still,

BEWARE OF DEAD-END JOBS THAT PAY WELL BUT LEAD NOWHERE.

any future careerworthy employer is going to wonder why Tim is entering the workforce as an entry-level candidate at age twenty-four and bringing no relevant experience or skills with him. Not an ideal platform from which to launch a career.

The lesson is clear. If you don't have a job after college, it's okay to move home while you look for meaningful employment. No future employer is going to fault you for that. Just make sure you use the time to develop a job search strategy. More importantly, if you do need to earn money in the process, find some kind of work that has transferable and marketable skills. Remember: even a job at Wendy's can teach you something about customer service.

IT'S NO VACATION

We have had many clients who have for one reason or another taken up temporary residence at home. There's no shame in it. In fact, more than at any time in recent decades, today's college-graduate children are more closely connected to their mothers and fathers. And parents, who twenty-five years ago would have been embarrassed to have a college graduate at home, now may welcome the prospect. Maybe it's because the whole process of learning to become an adult seems to take longer than it used to. Life's traditional mile markers—college, career, family, retirement—are more elastic than before. Four years of college have become five or even six. Couples marry older and have kids later. College graduates now enter the workforce for several years before applying to business or law schools. The rules are much more flexible than they used to be. But that doesn't mean they don't exist.

Fact number one: a parent's principal job is to raise children, not adults. And in their eyes, their job is pretty much over once their child graduates. Fact number two: one of the reasons you went to college in the first place was to give yourself the best possible chance of finding a good job. Your parents are letting you come home to help you do that. Fact number three: even though your parents may say you can stay for as long as you want, they're lying. Ultimately they need you to leave, to begin your own life. It's their job as parents.

Go home if you must, but use the time to think about why you're doing it, what you might want to do in the way of work, and what plan you have for making it happen. Most importantly, understand that job hunting takes planning and time. It isn't like writing a term paper or your summer reading. You can't save it till the last minute. Don't go home, take the summer off, and wait until Labor Day to begin prospecting. It'll put you three months behind the competition. While you're preparing your resume and setting up a network, your competition will be out interviewing for and getting the jobs you were looking for. Make a point of achieving something every day, however small or menial you think it might be. Write a thank-you letter, search a job database, add to your network. If your parents see you making an effort to find work, setting up interviews, sending out resumes, they're much more likely to stay off your back. That alone is worth its weight in gold.

YOU DON'T HAVE TO BE RICH TO LIVE ON YOUR OWN

Face it: most entry-level jobs pay between $35,000 and $40,000 per year. A lavish salary, certainly not. But a living wage, we think so.

Back in the seventies, an average starting salary was about $7,000. We'll save you the math. That's $134 per week or $3.36 per hour before taxes. Many student cell phone bills run more than that.

And, back in the seventies, parents didn't feel as positive about the notion of their recent college graduate returning home. Chances were, the bedroom had been turned into a sewing room and a favorite bell-bottom jumpsuit was sent to hang on a clothing rack at the Salvation Army. The point is, these college graduates found a way to live on their own despite salaries that today appear insultingly low.

Well, you say, that was then. Things were much less expensive than they are today. Sadly that's true, even factoring in inflation. But does that put your quest for independence out of reach? We don't think so. Today a not-so-fancy two-bedroom apartment in one of Boston's less glamorous neighborhoods might run about $1,100 a month—in Los Angeles or San Francisco, slightly more. You can't afford it by yourself, maybe, but with a roommate it's certainly doable. Look at the numbers. If you earn $35,000 a year, you'll have a net income of about $2,190 per month. Assume you can afford to pay about $550 (25 percent) of your monthly income for rent. Ditto your roommate. Guess what? You're there: $1,100. Yes, you may need to ask your parents for some help, work overtime, or borrow from savings to come up with the first month's rent and security deposit. But it will be worth the extra effort.

DON'T ASSUME YOU CAN'T AFFORD TO LIVE ON YOUR OWN.

We are making two points here: first, don't automatically assume you can't support yourself on an entry-level starting salary. It's done successfully every day. It might be tight and you certainly won't be living in the lap of luxury for a while, but you won't have to sell your blood to make ends meet, either. Point number two: maybe you think it's too expensive to live on your own because your expectations are too high. Consider lowering them. When we talk to students about the prospect of setting themselves up in an apartment, many of them insist on living alone. Maybe they have a boyfriend or girlfriend and want the privacy. Maybe they need a change from the sardine-can living of college. Who knows? But whatever the reason, the truth is that solo living is usually out of the grasp of most young adults.

Case in Point ➤ We had a client, **Amy Madigan**, who wanted to pursue a job in the communications industry. Her thinking, quite correctly, was that New York City was the only place for jobs of that kind. Amy, a graduate of an upstate New York college of communications, is smart, qualified, and determined. She was well prepared to begin her job search. And Amy's parents—quite generously, we thought—offered to pay her rent for at least six months or until she found a job. What did Amy do? Rather than stick with her plan to launch her career, she started looking for an apartment in a doorman building in midtown Manhattan, arguably the most expensive real estate in the country and possibly the world. We asked if she'd found anything she liked. She said, yes, she'd found a great place with a view of Gramercy Park. And it was only $2,350 a month.

Our advice to Amy was that if her parents signed that lease, we hoped they were prepared to support her for a long time. She would never come close to affording such luxury on a beginner's salary. We said she should focus on her job search strategy and find some roommates, two or more. Look across the river, maybe Williamsburg or Hoboken, where rents are more reasonable, and kiss your privacy good-bye for a while.

Happily for her and her parents, Amy found a great job at Hearst Publishing, and two roommates she really liked from *Craigslist*. They now rent a three-bedroom with a garden in Brooklyn and have a dog. Not Park Avenue, but affordable and a lot more fun. Amy's happy ending is not the exception.

Case in Point ➤ Taj Mira, a graduate of a prestigious college in Baltimore, is working in a well-known New York investment bank and lives in Manhattan with three other roommates from the same firm. They have a great apartment in a prewar building on the Upper West Side that none of them could afford on their own.

We know the world is an expensive place to live in. Remember, we live in it, too. But sometimes, it's easy to use the economy as an excuse to move back home. If being out on your own is something you really want to do, it's highly likely you can pull it off. We see it happen every day.

THE **TEN COMMANDMENTS**
OF MOVING BACK HOME

Okay, you've decided to move back home. You've asked your parents and they've said yes. Now what? Here are a few guidelines to make your stay at home more productive and enjoyable for you and your parents.

VI.
Watch out for go-nowhere jobs that provide money but no skills for advancement.

VII.
Help out with expenses where you can. It costs money to have you back home.

VIII.
Set weekly job search goals (e.g., mail five resumes, set up one interview).

IX.
Don't be invisible. Spend a little time with your parents; it's the least you can do.

X.
Remember how lucky you are to be welcomed back home. Not everyone is.

I.
Remember, it may be your home, but it's not your house—so help out.

II.
Ask your parents if you can move in. Tell them when you're moving out. Have a financial goal to meet.

III.
Thou shalt not freeload.

IV.
Living at home is a luxury. Treat it as such; it won't last forever.

V.
Keep your parents in the loop about what you're doing to find a job; it reduces the nag factor.

HOW CAN I LOOK FOR A JOB IF I DON'T KNOW WHAT I WANT TO DO?

THE CANDIDATE ILLUMINATION PROCESS

We'd love to be able to tell you that the smartest move you ever made was buying this book. We applaud your intelligence and good taste, of course. But the hard truth is that despite all the claims to the contrary, there is no publication, Web site, or career counselor whose advice can guarantee you the job of your dreams, this book included.

We can promise that the combination of our strategies, your hard work, and a healthy dose of your own personality should give you the confidence and the skills to kick some serious job-hunting butt. Believe it or not, you already possess many of the tools to make that happen. You have above-average intelligence and have been given, at someone's considerable expense, an outstanding education. We assume you have reasonably decent personal habits, don't have any typos on your resume or food in your teeth, and are bright enough to know you should wear clean clothes to your interviews.

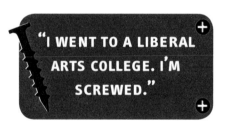

What you may not have is the confidence to put all this together in a package employers will find irresistible. That's what Candidate Illumination is all about. Its purpose is to provide you with the tools and strategies to help you be as good as you can be. It's that simple and that complex. When you know you're at the top of your game, confidence follows. And no matter what any "expert" tells you, confidence gets jobs.

In the following chapters we talk about every aspect of the job search process: how to find your focus when you're uncertain about what you want to do, the importance of creating your own personal brand, how to make your resume tell a story, and interview strategies that will give you the self-assurance to tell that story in the most compelling and memorable way. In the process we also hope you'll learn how to avoid the costly and unnecessary mistakes that keep qualified candidates from landing the jobs they want and deserve.

People are fond of saying that the sweetest words in the English language are "I love you." Personally, we think "I told you so" is a pretty strong contender. But to us, "When can you start?" walks away with the blue ribbon. The Candidate Illumination process, outlined in the following chapters, is all about helping you to help yourself get to that most desirable of moments: when your new employer shakes your hand and says, "You're hired."

FATHER DOESN'T ALWAYS KNOW BEST

For years, we've been approached at social gatherings by friends, acquaintances, and even clients. "Would you mind talking to my daughter [son]? She's graduating from college and doesn't have any idea what she wants to do. You must know someone who can get her a job." Multiply this conversation by a hundred every year, and you've got a great reason to stop going to cocktail parties.

It's clear from these conversations that there's widespread misunderstanding about how the world works when it comes to present-day job hunting. Parents still believe that little has changed since they set out to find their first job, so they give their children advice that's twenty years out of date. Often it's not only wrong, it's also harmful.

And college graduates, raised in the age of technology and instant communication, believe that all it takes is a well-prepared resume coupled with a little time on the Internet, and presto! Juicy offers will be delivered to their desktops.

It may take a month or two, but parents ultimately discover there's not really very much they can do to get jobs for their children. Bitter news to a generation of mothers and fathers who've devoted their lives to smoothing their kids' way to adulthood. And after posting a couple of hundred resumes and receiving little or no response, the

> **JUST BECAUSE YOUR FATHER HAS A JOB, IT DOESN'T MEAN HE'S AN EXPERT ON HOW TO GET ONE.**

newly graduated job seeker acknowledges that maybe the Internet isn't the Yellow Brick Road he thought it was. So now what?

If you've recently graduated and feel you can't begin serious job hunting until you have some inkling of what you might want to do with your life, you're not alone. Every year colleges disgorge tens of thousands of graduates who haven't the faintest idea of what to do next. It's the most common complaint we see. The anthropology major who doesn't want to live in Tasmania studying tribal ceremonies. The sociology major who has no interest in social work. The art historian who can't see herself working in museums for the rest of her life.

Where to begin?

In our experience as hiring managers, the candidates who have the easiest time finding employment have concentrated their efforts on one or two specific industries, can demonstrate competent knowledge about them, and can effectively project their interest in the company interviewing them. That's our idea of focus, and to us it's step one in every job search process. Where you look for it and how you find it are what this chapter is all about.

WHAT DO YOU HAVE TO SELL AND WHO WILL BUY IT?

"How can I look for a job when I don't know what I want to do?" is not a question you should be asking yourself. More to the point is "What have I got to sell, and who's most likely to buy it?" A psychology major who spent summers waiting tables on Nantucket may decide investment banking is where the bucks are, but he doesn't have a single qualification to make him desirable as a prospect. No finance courses, no accounting, no political science. He's wasting his own time and the employer's.

How do you go about finding out what you're good at, and what skills and resources do you have that might be of value and interest to a potential employer?

Take inventory. Begin by examining all your personality traits, good and bad. Are you really a hard worker, or do you just want people to think you are? Are you a self-starter, or do you leave everything until the last minute? Is money important to you, or is job satisfaction more compelling? Do you like high-pressure environments, or are you more comfortable in relaxed situations? Do you need the security that comes from working in large corporations, or do you thrive in smaller, more entrepreneurial surroundings? These are key questions, and you need to be brutally honest with yourself in answering them. They're determinants of your long-term job satisfaction and career success. If you hate pressure, rule out becoming a Wall Street bond trader, even if you're a math genius and love working with money. Maybe banking would be a safer choice. If you're shy and uncomfortable around people but enjoy managing data, stay away from sales and concentrate on analyst positions. Sounds pretty obvious, doesn't it? But we can't tell you how many job seekers, in their hunger to find employment, have gotten themselves into work situations they loathed because they didn't acknowledge their inner voices. Don't be like the candidate who took a job with a national insurance company, drawn to the mathematical modeling and demographic research they employed in evaluating risk, only to discover he was on the road four days a week hawking policies.

Dissect your work experience. Do you have specific skills acquired in the workplace that might interest an employer? Did your previous jobs or internships involve customer contact, handling money, working as part of a team? Did you learn how to use software programs specific to particular industries? Were you involved in projects that showcased your skills: organization, leadership, creativity? Did you initiate any projects on your own that benefited your employer? Set up a new filing system? Restructure store inventory? Reorganize the reference library or help write sales materials? Can you speak more than one language? If so, how fluently? These aren't just tasks you performed. They're demonstrations of your personal qualities. Qualities companies will pay for.

Think about who you are and what you stand for. Could you work for a cigarette company or a defense contractor? Do you see yourself as a caregiver? Which is more important: friends and family, or career success? If the answer is career success, how much are you willing to sacrifice to get it, and for how long? How flexible are you in terms of where you work? Do you want to stay close to home, or are you willing to follow the opportunities wherever they lead?

These are tough questions. Self-appraisals are always difficult and sometimes even painful. But make the effort. At the end, you'll walk away with a much better understanding of who you are, what you care about, and what you have to offer. Most importantly, you've taken the crucial first step in finding your focus.

LOOK FOR THE COMPANIES THAT ARE LOOKING FOR YOU

Now for the tough part. Instead of searching for companies you might like to work for, look for companies that value your skill set. If one of your strengths is customer service, find companies competing in a sector that places a premium on managing customer relations, like the hospitality industry. If you're a good salesman, seek out sales- or marketing-driven companies. In effect, you are looking for companies that are looking for your particular skills. At this stage, what a company makes or what specific service it offers should be less important in your decision process than the qualities required to be successful in the posted job openings.

How do you find such companies? Visit the job banks. They have countless open listings, and most of these are accompanied by detailed descriptions of the responsibilities and the skills required to assume them. Spend a day reading job descriptions and we guarantee some great things will happen. First, you'll end up feeling much better about your overall marketability. Hard as it may be to believe, there are actually companies out there looking for someone just like you. Second, by exploring the multitude of opportunities, you'll discover jobs and companies you never dreamed existed. And last, when you find companies that have fifty open job requisitions, you can bet they're on the move. Profitable and successful organizations have happy and motivated employees. A good place to start your search.

LOOK FOR A JOB, NOT A CAREER

Many recently graduated students labor under the misconception that in searching for a first job they're choosing a career they have to live with for the rest of their professional life. The weight of that decision paralyzes them. But as any experienced business-person knows, the search for a rewarding career is a non-linear process. It could involve a number of jobs and take a good many years to find. View an entry-level job as a first step in that exploration. It's a chance to gather information and experience, data that will eventually inform and guide your long-term career choice.

DON'T EXPECT YOUR DREAM JOB — OR SALARY — RIGHT OUT OF THE GATE.

What if the job doesn't work out and you find you hate it? At least you'll know what you *don't* want to do. That alone is a valuable lesson. But by being employed, you've also gained a broader understanding of how business works. You'll likely have been exposed to a whole range of new experiences, and you'll have proved to yourself and others that you're capable of the fundamental requirements of the workaday world: showing up on time, performing your assigned tasks professionally and within deadlines, writing memos, advising customers, participating in meetings, and so on. These simple yet vital building blocks of professional life are all marketable skills that will enhance your resume and bolster your confidence.

EVEN THE MOST MENIAL SUMMER JOB HAS VALUE

Take waiting tables, for instance. Not exactly a resume-builder, but valuable nonetheless. What interests employers is what you learned from the experience. Seen from that perspective, waiting tables is more than serving meals; it's also about dependability, customer service, working as part of a team, and managing money.

The same is true for college sports. We've seen thousands of resumes listing college sports participation under "Other Interests," alongside windsurfing and Ultimate Frisbee. Instead, think about what playing an organized sport might mean to a potential employer. It says teamwork, competitive spirit, and performance under pressure. It also says dependability, discipline, commitment, and hard work. If you were captain of a team, add leadership to the list. That's what's salable, and that's why so many companies seek out and hire student-athletes. For them, it's a safe bet.

FOCUS MALFUNCTIONS

Generally speaking, lack of focus is the most prevalent condition we see among first-time job seekers. And it doesn't seem to matter whether they think they know where they're headed or they haven't the

FOCUS MEANS NARROWING YOUR CHOICES.

faintest inkling. In our experience, these tend to fall into one of four groups:

- **Clueless:** "How can I choose when I have so many choices?"

- **Father knows best:** "My dad says . . ."

- **Tunnel vision:** "There's only one job for me, and if I don't get it, I'll just die."

- **Dreamer:** "I majored in math but I want to work with the Olympic ski team."

THE "CLUELESS" CANDIDATE

They have a broad range of interests, have done a variety of internships, may have studied abroad, and are willing to do just about anything, if they could only figure out where to begin. Clueless candidates have so many options and so many areas of interest that they find it impossible to choose among them.

Take **Tara Filkins** from Portland, Oregon, for instance. Tara is a poster child for postgraduation paralysis. She graduated from a small, prestigious college in Ohio, with a degree in philosophy because it sounded interesting and didn't require a thesis. She studied abroad for a semester, minored in mathematics, and wrote for the college literary magazine. She is bright, polished, beautiful, and she loves to travel. Sounds like a personal ad, doesn't it? Her philosophy studies gave Tara the ability to see complex issues from varying perspectives; her math studies, the ability to analyze and solve problems. She writes well and expresses herself clearly and concisely, with occasional moments of wit thrown in. On the face of things, Tara is well equipped to do almost anything she wants. And therein lies the problem: too many choices and not enough information to discriminate among them. In a desperate attempt to find clarity, she even took a couple of career aptitude/personality tests through her college career services department. Their conclusion: she'd be best suited for a position teaching English as a second language in a foreign country; Vietnam came to mind. Not exactly the advice she was looking for. No wonder Tara was daunted by the job search process. She didn't know where to begin because she'd spent too much time listening to other people and not enough time listening to herself.

We took Tara back to the basics. First, we told her to stop looking for the "perfect job." Given her state of confusion, she probably wouldn't recognize it anyway. Instead, we told her to ask herself three questions: What am I good at? What makes me happy? How can I put the two together?

It turned out that Tara had a variety of highly marketable skills she hadn't considered when looking for a job. Her summer work as a professional caterer had taught her how to work under pressure and under tight deadlines. Her time spent with clients gave her an understanding of the importance of superior client service and the necessity of knowing how to solve problems on the fly. What employer wouldn't consider these as assets?

What's more, Tara loved to cook and was good at it. And we're not just talking about rustling up a batch of cookies. Tara could plan and prepare highly sophisticated, complex dining experiences, complete with appropriate wines and table decor that any five-star restaurant would envy. And she did this all for the sheer love of it.

It didn't take a genius to recognize Tara was a perfect candidate for the hospitality business. What industry is more customer service–driven and places a higher premium on the ability to work under pressure? Moreover, it generates much of its revenue from catering and special events, putting Tara right in the middle of the action.

Why didn't Tara think of this herself? Because she saw her cooking/catering as a hobby, something she could do on her own time for her friends and family. In her mind, catering professionally meant she'd have to set up her own business, raise considerable capital, and work for years to build up a successful following. Not only did she not want to be an independent businesswoman, she also needed a paycheck, and sooner rather than later.

We urged Tara to clear her head and focus on the food and hospitality industries. We worked together to help her identify five premium hotels in the Boston area, hospitality organizations that would likely have an interest in her skill set and her considerable knowledge of food service.

Through her own efforts, she discovered that several of these hotels had catering-related jobs available. We helped her craft her story, wrote a resume that illuminated her assets, coached her on how to tell her story clearly and passionately, and sent her out into the world.

The result: she knocked them dead. Employers loved her experience, responded to her poise and sophistication, and readily understood Tara was not a candidate looking for just any job, but a young woman with a real passion for the food business. Tara is now in the executive training program for a major luxury hotel chain. She loves her job, and they love her.

The lessons learned? Tara focused her energies on a single industry in which her talents, proven abilities, experience, and academic perspectives were valued. Her enthusiasm definitely made her an intriguing prospect, but her focus got her the job.

THE "FATHER KNOWS BEST" CANDIDATE

These helicoptered candidates have been backseat-driven by their parents their entire lives. The result: they haven't developed the ability to find their own way. Faced with the unsettling prospect of launching themselves into the real world, father knows best candidates are particularly vulnerable to parents who want to micromanage their job search.

These are the candidates who've learned to do what they've been told: taken courses their parents thought important, involved themselves in parentally sanctioned extracurriculars, and sought summer jobs and internships parentally crafted to enhance their chances of being hired into "suitable" careers.

When it comes to looking for a job after college, father knows best candidates feel obligated to seek out a position their father or mother might deem worthwhile. It's not the job they really want, but it's what the parents think is right. The result: they become ambivalent and conflicted candidates whose lack of commitment is immediately evident to any experienced interviewer.

Case in Point ➤ "Father knows best" perfectly describes **Kip Meyers**. Kip went to a large private college in New Orleans, his father's alma mater. At his father's urging, he graduated with a business degree and bolstered his financial qualifications by completing additional coursework in accounting at a local university.

Somewhat against his parents' wishes, Kip also completed production and development internships at Warner Brothers and ABC. While in college, he became the business manager for the college radio station and freelanced on a local New Orleans entertainment Web site.

It was obvious to us that Kip's heart lay in entertainment. Kip's father thought differently. "Entertainment isn't a real career," he cautioned. "By the time you turn thirty you'll be burned out, and then what'll you do? Start over? Forget entertainment; be a banker. It's important work with a career path that will last you a lifetime. If you decide you don't like it, you'll at least have the skills to transfer to any industry you want."

Unconvinced, but honoring his father's wishes, Kip reluctantly started interviewing with banks. Not only did he not get a job offer, he didn't even make it to the second round of on-campus interviews.

In typical fashion, Kip's father decided to take over his son's job search. Banking interviews were arranged through family and business connections, some at very high corporate levels. But despite the quality of these connections, none of the companies showed any interest in Kip.

Kip's father called us, believing that if his son could only polish up his interviewing skills he could land a job at a respected financial institution. Just a few quick lessons and he'd be well on his way to a successful banking career.

When Kip came to us he was frustrated, had lost his confidence, and was really feeling the heat from his father. It was clear to us in fifteen minutes that Kip wasn't a banker. What he loved, where his real interest lay, was entertainment. Kip had already proved he was temperamentally suited to the demands of the industry. He was smart, high-energy, full of enthusiasm, and knew a lot about the business. And he learned about it not because someone had told him to but because he wanted to.

Kip's problem in finding a banking job had nothing to do with his skill set. He had the right degree, had taken the appropriate courses, and had even done well in them. But he wore his ambivalence and lack of passion for financial services on his sleeve, where every interviewer could see it.

We assured Kip that by focusing on the business side of entertainment, he could pursue the career he loved and still appease his father's desire to see his son in "a reputable line of work." His father reluctantly agreed. With his newly focused resume in hand, Kip immediately lined up interviews with major players in the broadcast industry. In less than three weeks he found the job of his dreams, as an assistant manager of business development for a major cable network in New York.

The moral of the story? If you want to find your dream job, make sure it's your dream and not somebody else's. Your parents may have the best of intentions for your future, but you're the one who has to show up for work every day. It's a lot easier to be successful if you're doing something you love. And isn't that what your parents would want for you in the first place?

THE "TUNNEL VISION" CANDIDATE

These hyperfocused individuals approach the job search interested in only one company or one job. If that job isn't available—or worse still, if they don't get it—the world comes crashing down around them.

Fear is usually the root cause of this myopia: fear of rejection, fear of failure, fear of the unknown. These candidates manage their anxiety by focusing on a single company they believe in, one they think will make them happy. And they pursue it relentlessly, almost always to the exclusion of all other possibilities.

This strategy creates a number of problems. First, it stops the networking process dead. From the tunnel vision candidate's perspective, why bother to build your network when you've already found your dream company? Second, since the prospect is often seeking one job, not the many available within the category, the odds of finding employment are drastically reduced. The candidate has set himself up for almost certain failure. And with it comes loss of confidence, breeding further failure. We call it the job-seeker death spiral.

Candidates who lose out on their dream jobs often simply give up. It's the "If I can't have the job I want, I don't want any job" syndrome.

Case in Point **Ted Grossman's** passion was helping people, particularly those less fortunate than himself. At a large midwestern university, he majored in psychology and spent his nonclassroom time running campuswide events to benefit abused children and women. He also interned with the Michigan Department of Social Services in Ann Arbor and volunteered at a local shelter for battered women. He spent his summers working as a counselor at a camp for underprivileged kids, managing their numerous athletic programs. We knew right away what Ted's first career move should be. Ted had made up his mind that he wanted to work in development and event planning for a charitable organization focused on helping abused children. He had no interest in working with sick, emotionally challenged, or underprivileged children, and he really didn't want to work in a hospital environment. To make matters worse, he'd settled on a single foundation that seemed to meet his exacting requirements, only to find out that they had no job openings. Ted was crushed, and by the time we met him, he had all but abandoned his job search.

By so restricting his "perfect job" requirements, Ted had effectively taken himself out of the running for exciting development positions in a variety of other significant philanthropic organizations.

Our first step with Ted was to bring him back to reality. We explained that a first job is exactly that: a first job, not a career. We reminded him that although he had some valuable experience, he still had a lot to learn about the philanthropic development process. By opening his mind to a wider variety of nonprofit institutions and organizations, he could gain valuable experience and greatly strengthen his resume. More importantly, we managed to convince Ted that by focusing on only one job he was wasting time and energy and setting himself up for inevitable disappointment.

Step one: Ted needed to broaden his focus. We settled on a list of ten organizations offering the kind of development experience Ted was looking for. We also urged him to expand his definition of target philanthropies to include any organization that served children. We also encouraged him to jump-start his job search by reaching out to several organizations simultaneously, juggling multiple leads rather than focusing on one job at a time.

Ted's "aha" moment came when he found himself in the enviable position of having five interviews in a single week, culminating in two job offers. He is now working in the development department of a national children's charitable organization and is part of a team responsible for raising millions of dollars each year for much-needed medical research.

The lesson: focus is fundamental to a successful job search, but hyperfocus can undermine a candidate's confidence and steal momentum from the process. Ted ultimately landed a job in an arena he previously would have deemed unsuitable, and discovered along the way that it offered the same challenges and "feel good" attributes he thought could come only from his dream company.

THE "DREAMER" CANDIDATE

What do you do with candidates who have invested most of their adult lives pursuing a single career, but decide after graduation that they want to work for a professional sports team?

Ask them about their qualifications for such a job and you get answers like "Well, I'm a real basketball junkie. I can name every starting player in the NBA. I know their stats, too." We hasten to point out that being a devoted fan doesn't qualify you for a position in the league organization.

While this example might sound extreme, we meet many candidates whose achievements are laughably out of synch with their expectations. Art history or anthropology majors with no relevant work or extracurricular experience, for instance, who, drawn by mind-blowing salary rumors, suddenly decide they want a career in investment banking. Earth to candidate: no possible way.

Kathryn McWilliams is a classic dreamer candidate. She graduated from a New York City college with a B.A. in business and a concentration in retail and fashion merchandising. Kathryn worked at various retail chains during her summers off, completed an internship as a teller at a local credit union, and did temp work at an accounting firm, doing spreadsheets and other data analysis.

When Kathryn came to Hayden-Wilder, we thought this was a no-brainer. Here is a young woman whose employment and internships were natural extensions of her coursework. It was obvious to us she was preparing for a career in the business side of retail.

And then came the shocker: Kathryn wanted to work for the New York Yankees. Why? Because she loved everything about the team, knew their stats and their win-loss record for the past three years, and could whip any guy in a Yankees trivia contest. On closer questioning, she grudgingly admitted that she had no experience in the sports or entertainment arenas; had never studied branding, marketing, or communications; and didn't even play sports. She worked out . . . occasionally.

Kathryn didn't care what she did in the Yankee organization—food vendor, ticket attendant, receptionist, promotions and advertising. She would even be a janitor as long as it was for the Yankees. They would have to hire her; after all, she was their number one fan. From her point of view, if *Seinfeld*'s bumbling George Costanza could work in the Steinbrenner organization, why couldn't she?

Kathryn obviously didn't have a prayer and she would have known that if she'd asked herself one all-important question: "Why should they hire me?" If she couldn't supply intelligent answers to that question, it was a surefire indication that she was chasing the wrong dream.

It took us a while to get her back on track. She didn't give up baseball without a fight, but over time she came to realize that passion alone was not enough; it takes both passion *and* solid qualifications to find the right job. More importantly, she realized that she had both these qualities in abundance if she refocused her energies in retailing. Her internships with major national clothing brands gave her valuable "on the floor" experience. And her banking background as a customer service specialist made her an excellent candidate for a career track position in the business and operations side of retail.

She could even concentrate on the merchandising side of the business, which might eventually lead her to working with the Yankees, Major League Baseball, or any number of other organizations that derive substantial revenues from licensed merchandise. In the short term, Kathryn came to understand that at least for the time being she would have to settle for just being another rabid Yankees fan.

It didn't take long for Kathryn to land a job with a major New York–based clothing manufacturer supplying men's and women's apparel to retail department chains and specialty stores. She works in the financial department, where she is able to get a broad view of the business and can use the skills she honed in her college business classes. Kathryn loves her job, is learning a lot, and attends Yankees games whenever she can get tickets.

What's the moral? First, fantasy careers cannot be manufactured out of whole cloth. They need to have some basis in reality. Second, however sincere one's passion, enthusiasm must be accompanied by skill sets that contribute to a company's bottom line; it's that simple. Find the organization that values your experience and will pay you for it and you're well on your way to finding your real dream job.

We've told you just about everything we know about focus. If you're a recent graduate who has no idea about how to begin the process of finding a rewarding job, start with finding your focus. It's where every serious job search begins. Ultimately it's nothing more complicated than finding out who you are and what you can do, and then searching for the company that wants to pay you for those skills.

BREAKING AWAY
FROM THE PACK

Chances are, if you've taken a marketing course in college, you know how important a brand is. And if you're one of the many grads who haven't studied marketing, you probably know how important a brand is anyhow. The United States is the most brand-conscious country in the world. American businesses spend billions of dollars a year developing and protecting brand images. We're exposed to brand names and brand stories from infancy to death, and through every important phase of our lives.

Your favorite clothing isn't generic. It's branded. Whether you are a fan of Abercrombie, Old Navy, Lily Pulitzer, Carhartt, Patagonia, Tommy Hilfiger, or Ralph Lauren, you are aware of what clothing brand you and your friends are wearing. What's more, you probably think the brand of clothing someone wears tells you a lot about what kind of person she is. Scary, isn't it?

WHAT IS A BRAND?

Whatis.com defines a brand as "a product, service, or concept that is publicly distinguished from other products, services, or concepts so that it can be easily communicated and usually marketed." The key word in this definition is "distinguished." Why? Because the whole purpose of a good brand is to set itself apart itself from its category competitors.

We believe that success in your job search is all about creating your own personal brand. It will generate the positive attention you'll need to get the job. It's all about making the sale. Why do Coke, Nike, Budweiser, UPS, BMW, McDonald's, and many others invest hundreds of millions of dollars each year promoting their brands? Because it works—see for yourself in the quiz on the following page.

But great brands are more than advertising taglines. They create emotional relationships between product and customer. It's called brand personality: Volvo isn't just another car, it's the safest car, and it's bought by people for whom safety is all-important. A Mercedes-Benz boasts the quality of German engineering; its personality: luxurious,

1. What is the main color on the Coke can/label?

2. What is the Nike logo?

3. What beverage is the King of Beers?

4. Which company has the line "What Can Brown Do For You?"

5. What is the "Ultimate Driving Machine"?

6. What do you think of when you see the Golden Arches?

Answers: 1. Red; 2. Swish; 3. Budweiser; 4. UPS; 5. BMW; 6. McDonald's.

dependable, long-lasting. And BMW is for people who love to drive; it sells youth, energy, excitement, adventure.

Another aspect of great brands is consistency. Every product in the above brand quiz has maintained a constant image over time, and done it in some cases for decades. Why are they part of our psychic DNA? Because we've heard them and seen them over and over for years. Repetition is the secret of their memorability. Show us a brand that redefines itself every couple of months and we'll show you a brand that, for all intents and purposes, doesn't exist.

What does all this mean as you set out to create your own brand?

1. You need to create a unique story to tell that reflects who you are.

2. That story must clearly resonate with the customer (the employer).

3. The message should be consistent, regardless of the audience.

4. Use your network as your communication medium.

PERSONAL BRAND STORIES

A good brand story communicates the product's benefits, is unique and persuasive, talks to a specific audience in an appealing way, and ultimately triggers a sale. If that isn't a perfect description of a successful job search campaign, we don't know what is.

Why is a strong brand story so effective in gaining the attention of prospective employers? Because most interviewers are bored to death by the sameness of the answers they get to their interview questions. Imagine how refreshing it is to meet candidates offering clear messages about their value as future employees. What better way to set yourself apart from the also-rans.

Putting yourself in the spotlight may sound easy. It's not. For your entire life, you've worked hard to fit in, to have friends who share similar interests, and to avoid being labeled a "freak." Now that you've graduated from college, those days are over. Suddenly it's not about fitting in anymore; it's about standing out. And for many of you it's an uncomfortable transition. But get over it. A successful job search is all about being different. You need to learn how to talk about yourself to total strangers, and to do it in a compelling and consistent way.

THINK OF YOURSELF AS A BRAND.

THAT'S MY STORY, AND I'M STICKING TO IT

Why is consistency so important? Imagine being a fly on a wall for a moment. You're listening to people at a cocktail party talk about Patty Samuels. Most of the people in the room know who Patty is. She's recently graduated from a prestigious private southern university with a double major in English and anthropology. Patty's name has come up in conversation and you listen to a few of the guests' comments:

"I hear Patty graduated from college and has decided to go to grad school."

"I thought Patty was going to law school."

"I hear she is taking a year off to travel."

"I don't think so; she was an English major and will probably end up working for a newspaper."

"Someone told me Patty was moving to New York."

"I got the impression she just wanted to get a job. Any job. So she could get out of the house and live on her own."

Wow. Five different people with five different versions of her plans. Not exactly a consistent brand story.

Instead, imagine that those same five people were talking about Patty because they knew her brand story:

"I hear Patty graduated from college."

"I know, she is planning on moving to New York to land a job in journalism."

"She'd be great working for a magazine or newspaper—she had internships with Vogue *and the* Washington Post.*"*

"She loves to write and seems to understand the business she's getting into. Good for her!"

"My brother-in-law is an editor for Time *magazine. I should introduce Patty to him."*

The differences between the two conversations are stunning. In the second, it is very clear she has taken *control of* what is being said about her. Everyone is grounded in what she is doing. They can talk about her and share the same brand messages. In effect, these people become brand advocates, or salespeople, for Patty.

As Patty networks and meets more people, she is building a sales force for her own personal brand. She is telling her story over and over, just as BMW and UPS do. And the more her story is heard, the more likely she is to uncover a good lead or an introduction that will move her toward landing the job she wants.

HOW CAN I CREATE MY OWN BRAND STORY?

If you think of the typical ads you see in magazines, there are usually three components:

1. a headline (to catch your attention)
2. body copy (describing the product or service)
3. a tagline (with a call to action)

These elements are then enhanced by engaging graphics and visuals.

Now think about your own brand story. We're not advocating creating an ad for yourself. But if you think about your brand story as having a headline, body copy, and tagline, it will definitely help.

Your **headline** is a quick, captivating introduction. It should answer the questions *"Tell me about yourself"* or *"What are you up to these days?"*

Your **body copy** should include key facts you want your networking contact to know. It answers the questions *"Why do you want to go into [journalism]?"* or *"What interests you about [journalism]?"*

Your **tagline** is the final thought you want to leave with your contact. It's your call to action. It answers the questions *"Is there anything else you'd like me to know?"* or *"Is there anything I can do?"*

CONTROL WHAT PEOPLE THINK ABOUT YOUR BRAND

It's important to remember your audience. Be sure to write your brand story so it appeals to potential networking contacts as well as potential employers. For example, if someone asks you *"Tell me about yourself,"* you can be sure that person doesn't want to know where you were born, where you went to high school, or how many brothers and sisters you have. She wants to know why she should be interested in you from an employment perspective.

Which is the more powerful response to *"Tell me about yourself"*?

1. *"I was born in Omaha and my family moved to Lincoln when I was in high school. It was really cold in Nebraska, and my older brother went to Florida State University, which he really liked, so then I decided I wanted to go to college in the South. I just graduated, so I'm looking for a job."*

Or

2. *"I just graduated from college with a degree in English and anthropology and I'm looking for a job in journalism in New York."*

There's no question that the second response is much better; it grounds the conversation, gets right to the point, and lets the candidate begin to control the networking/interviewing process. The second answer is *relevant* to the networking contact or interviewer.

Now try the body copy. Again, think about the audience and think about what matters to them as a networking contact or potential employer. Here are two answers to the question *"Why do you want to be in journalism?"*

1. *"You know, I loved being an English major and I'm a great writer, so I really want to work someplace where I can start writing right away, because I think I'm beyond being an assistant. Plus I'm good with people, which will help me when I have to interview people for articles and things."*

Or

2. *"Well, I was fortunate enough to have had internships at* Vogue *and the* Washington Post, *and I really like the business. I love to write and edit, and my professors and employers told me I'm good at it."*

If you examine these answers from the perspective of a networking contact or employer, there's no doubt that the second answer is much stronger. The first answer is all about the candidate. Remember, you're laboring under the label of the entitlement generation; the first answer justifies this label. Also, the first answer includes statements that can't be quantified. How great a writer are you? How do you know? How do you know you're better than an assistant? What's more, this answer includes the lightweight statement employers hear ad nauseam: *"I'm good with people."* Whatever you do, don't say it. If you aren't good with people, you should be interviewing for work as a toll taker on an interstate highway, as a prison guard in a solitary-confinement unit, or as a technician in a testing facility with only lab rats as company.

The second answer tells us a lot about the candidate. This candidate really has her act together. She charts the beginnings of a career path, through her internships. She quantifies her talents in writing by citing praise from teachers and employers. And most importantly, she proves, in two short sentences, that she is focused and ready to launch her career.

Now comes the hard part. What's your tagline, your call to action? What do you want your networking contacts to do? How are you going to keep their attention? You certainly don't want them to blow you off. So you need to have a comeback to the classic blowoff *"That's interesting. If I think of anything, I'll let you know."*

Remember, you're developing a brand story to generate interest in your candidacy. You want lots of people to know your story and share it consistently and enthusiastically. And if you really boil it down, you want *help* from everyone you meet. Unfortunately, people sometimes shy away from helping people with their careers; they don't like feeling obligated.

So instead of asking for help, ask for *advice.* There's nothing more flattering than being asked for advice. Advice can be received from people from all walks of life. Most people believe sharing advice is much safer than taking responsibility to help someone with his job search—and a lot less work.

WHAT IS YOUR TAGLINE, YOUR CALL TO ACTION?

Your tagline could be any of these:

"I'd love to meet for a cup of coffee and get your advice on my search."

"I really respect your opinion and would love to get your advice. May I call you at the office and book twenty minutes of your time?"

"Would you be willing to share some advice with me? I'm happy to meet you at your office."

All of these taglines represent a clear call to action. They also put the follow-up responsibility on you, so it makes it easy for the networking contact to say "yes."

Now it's time to put it all together. Imagine you're attending a cocktail party at your neighbor's house and you run into a colleague of your father's. Are you ready? Here's how our client Patty handled herself:

"Hi, Patty. Welcome home. It's great to see you. What are you up to?"

"Hi, Mr. Michaels. Great to see you, too. I've just graduated from college, with a degree in English and anthropology. I'm looking for a job in journalism, and I'm planning to move to New York."

"Terrific. Why journalism? I understand it's awfully competitive."

"Well, I don't know if my parents told you, but I was fortunate enough to have had two great internships, at Vogue *magazine and the* Washington Post, *while I was in college, and I just love the business. I also really like to write and edit, and my professors and*

employers told me I'm good at it. I just think it would be the perfect field for me."

"Super. Sounds like you've given it a lot of thought. Anything I can do to help?"

"I'd love to get your advice on my search. I don't mean right now at the party. May I call you at the office and set up twenty minutes to meet?"

"Absolutely, Patty. Call and book in time with my assistant."

PRACTICE, PRACTICE, PRACTICE

The best ads for the most popular brands in America do a great job of capturing the attention of their target audience. These ads tell a story in an entertaining, natural, emotional, comical, or factual way. They are sincere and believable. They are truthful and credible. They make the audience want to know more, or be entertained some more. These are ads that are talked about at work and at parties. These are ads that are memorable. They successfully sell products and services.

Great ads are successful due to a lot of hard work. A great ad takes time to craft and involves the talent of art directors, cameramen, stylists, directors, producers, editors, actors, and musicians. It requires a lot of "takes" and editing before the finished product is ready to roll.

Your brand story is to you what an ad is to a commercial product or service. You have to work hard on it, just as though you had a team working with you. It has to be spot on. It has to be real. You have to share your story in the most compelling way possible. There's a lot riding on your brand story, so it's important you try it out on a few trusted friends and family members before you go "public."

Ask yourself if you know your brand story cold. Are you comfortable telling your brand story? If you're not, practice in front of a mirror, or while you're driving the car. Next, ask yourself if your story sounds natural and not robotic. When you're convinced you can share your brand story in an easy, engaging fashion, you are ready to go.

BE TRUE TO YOUR BRAND

Have you ever heard someone say something like "I'd never buy a car from that dealer, their ads are so cheesy"? In fact, the dealer may be perfectly reputable and offer the same car selection as others. The problem is that their brand story wasn't convincing and left the customer looking at the competition across the street.

Case in Point We worked with a client, **Jeffrey Wolff**, an economics and psychology double major from a highly ranked midwestern college, who faced a similar situation. Jeffrey came to Hayden-Wilder convinced he wanted to be in the financial services industry because of his background in economics. Financial services paid more than other industries, and Jeffrey wanted to make money right away.

When it was time to develop Jeffrey's brand story, he opted to abandon many of his personal brand attributes. Instead, he favored tailoring a story that would resonate with a financial services firm. Jeffrey had completed an internship as an assistant to a bank economist, which he told us he really didn't enjoy, even though he had learned a lot. He also worked with a social anthropologist, researching the buying habits of women with preschool children. He loved his research internship because he could see firsthand "what made people tick." He was intrigued by what motivated people in the decision-making process.

Jeffrey's brand story focused on finance and banking but barely touched on his other experience. He networked and shared his story. Jeffrey landed a position as an assistant on a trading desk for a major brokerage firm.

About three months after Jeffrey started his job, he called us to say he was miserable. He realized he had abandoned many of his real interests and determined the trading world was not for him. He did, however, love the customer interface and the problem-solving he was exposed to daily.

We worked with Jeffrey to retool his brand story to incorporate *all* his experience and interests. He focused his search on companies with great reputations for customer service, an area in which he excelled. Jeffrey now works as a customer service representative at a major furniture manufacturer. He loves his job and has been fast-tracked into a management training program.

YOUR BRAND IS YOUR BIGGEST ASSET

Many companies place a monetary value on their brands and brand assets. Professionals who specialize in brand valuation have become trusted advisers to CEOs and CFOs. Some of the largest corporate acquisitions of the past decade have commanded huge price tags because their brand names and reputations were considered extremely valuable. Companies such as Google, Facebook, Oxygen, and AOL all fit this profile.

Your personal brand is equally valuable. Take a page from the pros and remember the following:

- Distinguish your brand from the competition.
- Understand your brand attributes.
- Make your brand relevant to your target audience.
- Develop a compelling brand story.
- Share your brand story consistently and frequently.
- Believe in your brand.

The more you work to build and protect your personal brand, the more your brand will deliver for you throughout your search process.

The best brands in the world evolve with their customers' needs, yet stay true to their core values. You'll find that the same thing will happen to you. Brand "you" will always have the same attributes, but you will grow and expand your brand offerings and competencies. By developing a personal brand now, you'll be rewarded in your current job search; and your personal brand will be the basis for your entire career.

THE LIGHTWEIGHT STATEMENTS EMPLOYERS HEAR AD NAUSEAM

"I'M GOOD WITH PEOPLE."

"I'M A HARD WORKER."

"I'M WELL ORGANIZED."

"I'M A SELF-STARTER."

"I'M GOOD AT MULTITASKING."

"I'M DEDICATED."

"I REALLY LIKE YOUR COMPANY."

I LOVE THE
BUILDINGS YOU
BUILD, THEY'RE
SO EYESTRIKING

To Whom It May Concern:

I am writing this letter because I am applying for a job you have that I saw in the *Boston Globe*. My name is Richard McElway, and I am very interested in finding out about it.

I know you do real estate and I don't know too much about that but I've been walking around Boston and keeping my eyes out for some of the things you've done. There seems like there's a lot, so I guess you are a pretty big company and that's good because you probably have lots of openings. Anyway, I just wanted to say that I love the buildings you build, they're so eyestriking and I hope you'll call me on my cell if you like my resume and would like to meet.

Sincerely,
Richard McElway

You've never met Richard McElway. We know, because we made him up. But the letter (it's really an e-mail) is real. Do you think the person who wrote this is smart? Do you want to read his resume? Would you like to meet him? Would you offer him a job? I hope you answered "No to all of the above." We sure would.

This cover letter, and many more like it, is a sad demonstration of the writing quality we see every day. And they don't come from graduates of some "nobody's ever heard of it" community college, either. They're written by students from among the most well-regarded educational institutions in the country. And quite frankly, letters like these really piss us off.

> **SOME GRADUATES FROM EVEN THE MOST PRESTIGIOUS UNIVERSITIES HAVE TERRIBLE WRITING SKILLS.**

Forget that it breaks just about every cover letter writing rule in the book. That's a subject for another chapter. What is so upsetting is that we think college-graduate communication skills—reading, writing, and speaking—are on the endangered species list. And you can't pin this one on the entitlement generation. This problem belongs squarely at the feet of high schools and colleges.

Forgive us if we go on a bit of a rant here. When you meet people you don't know, or read something they've written,

IGNORE PROPER GRAMMAR AT YOUR PERIL.

what is the primary method you use to judge their intelligence and education? Command of the language. If they're well spoken and/or know how to write, you'll assume they're reasonably intelligent. If not, you'll think they're stupid. That's how important language is. And we feel that our schools, from grade school through college, have really dropped the ball on this one.

Every parent has the right to expect that by senior year in high school his or her child will be capable of writing a grammatically correct sentence that can clearly express the intended thought. In our view, basic writing should be a prerequisite of graduation. Unfortunately, it's not. And apparently colleges don't lend much importance to it either, because year after year we see them unleash an army of graduates with limited practical writing skills.

In a recent study conducted by the outplacement firm Challenger, Gray, and Christmas, nearly half (47 percent) of executives surveyed said entry-level candidates need to have better writing ability. That makes bad writing more than a problem; it's a full-blown epidemic.

What does "better writing" mean? At minimum, all high school students, much less college grads, should understand the elements of grammar and sentence structure. They should know the function of paragraphs and how and when to use them. And most importantly, they should have a grasp of how to organize their thoughts on a page so the person reading it has some idea of what they're trying to say. Basic stuff. So basic it seems all but forgotten by many students and faculty alike.

Over the years, we've read thousands of resumes, cover letters, and thank-you notes from job candidates. And some of them are so poorly written we wonder how these kids managed to get through school. The most common errors:

1. run-on sentences

2. too few paragraphs

3. improper comma use

4. homonym errors (using "their" when you mean "they're")

5. subject/pronoun agreement ("everyone wants their kid to succeed")

These are the kinds of mistakes one expects to see from eighth- and ninth-graders, not college grads. And in our view our educational institutions should be ashamed of themselves for letting it happen.

So if everyone agrees that good writing is in short supply, why do our schools let it continue? First, grammar and syntax are poisonously boring. Students don't want to learn it, and instructors don't want to teach it. For an undergraduate, attending a grammar class is considered hard time, the educational equivalent of breaking rocks in a prison yard. So schools tend to give it minimum attention as part of the curriculum.

GRAMMAR AND SYNTAX ARE BORING. TOO BAD, MASTER THEM ANYWAY.

Second, people who are well read tend to be more articulate writers. And as any librarian, newspaper publisher, or bookstore owner will tell you, this generation—compared to its predecessors, anyway—reads very little.

Third, teachers, particularly at the college level, don't insist on proper grammar in grading student papers. Maybe they don't feel they have the time, maybe it's too boring, or maybe they feel it's not their job. So they don't penalize improper grammar and syntax with lowered grades. How a professor can hand out an A when the work is riddled with grammatical errors is beyond us. In any case, we've seen a lot of student papers demonstrating college-level thinking but high school (or lower) writing.

And, of course, text messaging and e-mail have further dumbed down writing skills to a hip code language.

The picture isn't totally bleak. There are "points of light." Babson College, a business school in Wellesley, Massachusetts, has a writing center established to help students who want to improve their skills, or who are directed to do so by the faculty. Hooray—it's about time.

WHAT YOU CAN DO RIGHT NOW TO BE A BETTER WRITER

It may seem we're trying to ram a lecture on writing down your throat. But the hard truth is, if your writing abilities are substandard, it won't matter who's to blame. You will suffer the consequences, and they can plague you throughout your career. You won't get the jobs you want. You'll be promoted more slowly and be paid less. And your bosses will steer you away from the most prestigious clients or the most important projects.

No one's expecting eloquence, just clarity. If you can't write well enough so others understand what you mean, you're not of much use to your employer. So if your writing skills aren't what they should be, fix them now, before you start the job search process. Take a practical writing course, find a good tutor,

> **YOUR WRITING SKILLS (OR LACK THEREOF) WILL AFFECT YOUR ENTIRE CAREER.**

or go online and take advantage of the many available writing sites. (Don't get involved with creative writing; it's for authors and journalists, not businesspeople.)

Last, learn how to organize and present your ideas. It's every bit as important as proper grammar. Burn these three words into your brain; they're the Magna Carta of effective business writing:

Focus. Presumably you have a reason for writing a particular document. Keep it in sight, and don't let your prose wander too far from home. If you do, you'll lose your reader for sure.

Clarity. Some writers try so hard to sound brilliant that no one can understand what they're trying to say. Overly complex sentence structures, pretentious vocabulary, using six words when one will do are the villains here. If you're writing an important document, take the time to show it to some colleagues. If they don't know what you're talking about, no one else will, either.

Brevity. In a business environment, brevity is next to godliness. Apply it to anything you write—e-mails, memos, cover letters, thank-you notes. If it's too long, it won't get read. And if no one reads it, you've wasted your time writing it.

We're sure you're all good writers and none of what we've been saying in this chapter applies to you. But just remember you're not in college anymore, so please don't write as though you are. You're not being graded, there's no teacher to impress, no word-count minimums. Keep the focus, clarity, and brevity commandments in your head and you'll find they'll do wonders for your writing style. Do you want the respect of your colleagues and superiors? Becoming a strong writer is the fastest way we know of to get it.

LET'S TALK E-MAIL ETIQUETTE

Here's our collective wisdom on e-mails. It's the greatest communication tool since the invention of the telephone. Everybody loves it, everybody uses it (we know a ninety-year-old great-grandmother with an e-mail address), and happily it has become accepted in business circles as a legitimate form of communication. That means that if you've just had an interview and want to send a thank-you note, an e-mail is a perfectly proper way to do it.

But when it comes to writing e-mails to prospective employers, there are certain rules, and you ignore them at your peril.

Sanitize your e-mail address. College is over, so your slammin' e-mail address that all your friends thought was so cool doesn't really cut it in the business world. Somehow we don't think you want *"hotrocks961@xyzmail.com"* to be the first thing an employer sees at the top of your resume. Change it *now*, before you forget.

Don't leave the subject line blank. It's not unusual for harassed executives to get as many as 150 e-mails a day, so they'll delete or not open anything looking like spam. A blank subject line in the message header is a sure spam tip-off. That's why many companies have fire-walls or filters to automatically erase unidentified correspondence. And unopened or rejected mail doesn't bounce back, so you'll never know it didn't get there. You don't want an employer to drop you from consideration, thinking you didn't have the courtesy to write a thank-you note. So play it smart. Always title your messages, even if it's only "Thanks."

Avoid overly familiar e-mail greetings. Simply put, if you're writing an e-mail to your "elders and betters," particularly if you don't know them, don't begin your message with "Hi, Bill," or any other informal greeting. It's the quickest way we know to get a relationship off on the wrong foot.

Use the same standards you'd apply to letter writing. You wouldn't begin a cover letter with "Hi." Don't use it in your e-mails, either. Even though it might seem a little old-fashioned, you can never go wrong by starting any e-mail with the old standby "Dear."

And be sure to be careful about first names. You'll have to use your judgment about when it's okay to use someone's first name and when it's not. But if

E-MAILS ARE BUSINESS LETTERS; TREAT THEM THAT WAY.

you're not sure, err on the side of caution and use title and last name (e.g., "Mr. Smith"). A little formality at the beginning of a relationship never hurts. We always say, "Never use superiors' first names until you're invited . . . at least twice. The first time they probably didn't mean it."

Keep your e-mails short. Want to really annoy your potential employers? Send a two-page e-mail. They won't be able to hit the "delete" key fast enough. E-mails are designed to speed up communication. Don't gum up the works with long-winded messages that no one will read.

Capitalize and punctuate. An e-mail is a letter. Treat it like one. Nothing is quite so unprofessional as a message that doesn't use correct punctuation or capitalization. It makes you look lazy and disrespectful. It may have been acceptable in college text messages, but it's not in business.

Check everything before you hit "send." Once you push the "send" button, your message is out of your control. You can never call it back. So check your e-mails carefully. Did you spell the recipient's name correctly? Are there any grammatical errors? Is the tone appropriate? Did you spell-check it? Most importantly, if you're writing a reply, should it go only to the sender, or everybody on the "cc" list? There have been a lot of ashamed red faces caused by inappropriate reply e-mails sent in error. Also, don't forget the attachments. If you say you're attaching your resume, make sure you do. It's easy to forget and embarrassing when you do.

Avoid e-mail hysterics. Unless the person to whom you're writing is having her car towed, never use the "urgent" flag. This is for messages that are time-critical. We don't think that applies to thank-you notes and the like. Ditto using all caps for emphasis, or multiple exclamation points or question marks. That's kid stuff and doesn't belong in a professional message.

Spell-check is not always your friend. Spell checkers have helped a lot of miserable spellers sound at least partially literate. But everybody who uses it has at least one horror story. Here's the rule. Just because spell-check says it's right doesn't mean it is. This applies not only to e-mail but to everything you write. The poem on the previous

SPELL CHECKER BLUES (A POEM)

Eye halve a spelling chequer
It came with my peace sea
It plainly marques for my revue
Miss steaks eye kin not sea
Eye strike a key and type a word
And weight four it two say
Whether I am wrong or write
It shows me strait a weigh
As soon as a mist ache is maid
It nose be four two long
And eye can put the error rite
Its rarely ever wrong
Eye have run this poem threw it
I am shore your pleased two no
Its letter perfect in its weigh
My chequer tolled me sew.

—Anonymous

page, by an unknown author, says it all.

That's about it on e-mailing. Your best rule of thumb? Treat every outgoing e-mail message the way you would a regular business letter. If you're not sure what those rules are, there's a ton of information on the Internet to help you.

HOW YOU SPEAK SPEAKS VOLUMES

"So, like I went to, you know, client services, and they like told me that I was so not ready to look for a job but if I wanted to like use job databases, that like Monster and Careers.com were ginormous ones. I have a friend that got a totally awesome job from one of them. So I asked her about like her resume and she goes, 'I did it online.' So I go, 'Like do you know the name of the site?' She went, 'Nope, but like I can find out.'"

We had a client who said "like" so often in her conversation that we started charging her a dime each time she used it improperly. In the course of forty-five minutes, she owed us $9.70. When she hit $10.00, we stopped counting. Did we cure her of the habit? Probably not. But we hope that she is now aware of what had become an unconscious and very damaging pattern of speech.

KNOW WHEN TO STOP TALKING.

Why the big deal? Let's assume you have an important interview and you want to make a good impression on your interviewers. If the first sentence out of your mouth makes you sound like some high-school sophomore talking on her cell phone to her girlfriend at the mall, you'll make an impression, all right, but not the kind you had in mind. Whether it's fair or not, people make judgments about your intelligence and education based on the way you speak. Sound stupid and people will think you are. Simple as that. On the other hand, we've known lots of not-so-bright people (we've even worked for a few) who get away with it because they present themselves well.

When we were in the advertising business, we knew a very talented and hardworking account executive who worked on one of our major pieces of business. She was thorough, smart, detail-oriented, and a terrific team player. Clients loved her. So did everyone in the agency. No one was more ready for promotion to account supervisor.

One problem. She talked like a teenage intern, totally undermining her considerable abilities. She didn't end up getting the promotion, although everyone agreed she deserved it. Why? Because her boss felt client senior management would be offended to have someone so young and seemingly inexperienced assigned to their account. Her boss decided it wasn't worth the risk.

Sounds unfair, doesn't it? Well, it probably is, but it points out one of the differences between college and the business world. In college, every student is presented with the same opportunities. The playing field is as level as the schools can make it. In business, you succeed because of the impression you make on your superiors. Everyone is vying for the boss's approval, and your speaking skills have the potential to be your secret weapon . . . or your worst enemy.

The way you speak and write will affect whether you are hired, if and how quickly you get promoted, and often how an entire task or project is judged. You can be smart as hell, put in sixty-hour workweeks, and be the best-liked person in the office, but none of that matters if you can't communicate effectively.

Now, most people reading this will probably say, "If I were in an interview, I'd never talk like that." Perhaps not. But interviews can be nerve-racking experiences. When applicants get nervous, they tend to lapse into familiar speech patterns, or to inject fillers ("you know," "um," or "like") to buy time while they think about how to answer a question. Everybody does it from time to time, but an interview should not be one of those. Fortunately, the more time you put into

LEAVE "LIKE," "YOU KNOW," AND "UM" AT THE DOOR.

preparing for an interview, the less likely you will be to fall back into these bad habits.

Here are a few tips to help you speak more fluently:

Speak slowly. Your mind may be racing and your heart jumping out of your chest, but if you take a deep breath and make a conscious effort to slow yourself down, you'll be amazed at how it will calm the butterflies. Not only that, it also will make it easier for your interviewer to understand what you're saying. Try it; it works.

Answer the question, then stop talking. Too many interviewees keep talking long after they've stopped thinking. Like talking too fast, it's a nervous habit. Don't do it. You'll bore the socks off your interviewer and get yourself into situations you can't talk your way out of. To paraphrase a Mark Twain quote, "Better to remain silent and be thought stupid, than to speak and confirm it."

Learn to pause. You're not a radio announcer, so a little dead air in an interview is okay. No hiring manager is going to fault you for spending a moment or two before you answer his or her question. It will make you appear thoughtful. It's much more effective than repeating "you know," "I mean," and "um" over and over.

Modulate your voice. If you want to show enthusiasm and passion about something, sound that way. I know your mind is racing, thinking about how to answer the question, but save a few brain cells for your delivery. Nothing sounds quite so unbelievable as an applicant talking about something she loves as though she's reading the fine print on a cell phone contract.

Practice, practice, practice. None of what we've told you will happen if you wait until the interview to put it into effect. Try to strike up conversations with your parents' friends or some other "superior," and practice speaking slowly, clearly, and with enthusiasm. When you're driving, ask yourself a typical interviewer's question (e.g., *"Tell me about yourself"*) and then listen to yourself answer it. If you like what you hear, chances are your audience will, too.

That's the end of our speech about writing and speaking. I hope you don't think we've nagged you too much. We know it's not easy to change the way you write or how you speak. After all, you've been doing both for most of your life. But if you make the effort to improve, there are few things you do that will prove as worthwhile or have a greater positive effect on your career.

IT'S NOT ABOUT WHAT YOU'VE DONE, BUT WHAT YOU CAN DO

We feel sorry for any person seeking outside advice these days on how to create a proper resume. If the thirty-six million Google hits we got to the key words "resume writing" is any indication, the world is filled with experts. And all of them either suggest or brazenly state that their format is guaranteed to generate top-quality interviews. "How to write a masterpiece." "Flawless resumes." "Seven tips for perfect resumes." "Ten tips for effective resume writing." And our personal favorite, "Hot tipes [sic] for resume writing." (Don't let the typo concern you; we're sure they're consummate professionals.)

RESUME GIMMICKS ARE LIKE TOUPEES, EVEN THE GOOD ONES ARE EASY TO SPOT.

What's scary here isn't that there are so many different sources of information on the subject; it's that almost every site recommends a different approach. But most of them are crap. In our estimation, the only feature they have in common is that they all contain, with varying degrees of clarity, chronological listings of jobs held and tasks performed. That's it.

Of course, there are countless suggestions for a multitude of graphic formats: rules; no rules; photos; borders; wallpaper effects; colored paper; typeface recommendations; and, most recently, the addition of the videotape resume. They're all calculated to improve your chances of catching an employer's eye. Not only do these gimmicks not work, they can also negatively dispose an employer toward the candidate using them.

Of the many hiring managers we've recently polled, the majority (67 percent) say that the bulk of resumes they see do not effectively communicate the strengths of the candidates. Their most common complaints: too long, too generic, no point of view, no story to tell, no focus. Our thoughts exactly.

Any company posting an open entry-level position is likely to receive hundreds of inquiries from prospective candidates—more if the posting has appeared on one of the major job sites, such as Monster or Careerbuilders.com. And most interviewers we know use the same draconian screening method to separate wheat from chaff: a quick once-over (twenty seconds or less), then sort into one of three piles: "yes" (always the smallest), "no," and "maybe." The "yes" pile then gets a subsequent screening. If the employer feels there are enough qualified candidates from that pile to fill the position, the "maybe" pile never gets looked at again. Where do these rejected resumes go? The "no" pile gets trashed, and the "maybe" pile is filed. "Filed" is business-speak for the place elephants go to die.

Get the point? You don't have a lot of time to state your case, so a poorly organized and poorly written resume is the equivalent of a typo in a cover letter or bad breath in an interview. It's the rabies of job-hunting: almost always fatal.

THE LOWDOWN ON LYING

There's a common misconception among recent graduates that a professionally prepared resume, whatever that is, is the secret to getting good interviews. From a content perspective, perhaps that's true. But watch out for that term "professionally prepared"—it can bite you in the ass. Resume designers make their money by charging you a fee for their services. It can range from $50 up to several thousand. Their interest is volume. Their mantra is: bring in a new customer, do the resume, get the cash, find another new customer. It's a sales-driven process.

LIE ON YOUR RESUME. GO TO JAIL. THAT'S THE LAW.

They don't care what your c.v. (*curriculum vitae*) says. All they're after is your approval. They need it to get paid. That's why some unscrupulous firms will inflate your qualifications or give you credentials you don't really have. They'll tell you it's not a problem. It's okay, they'll say, to call yourself an assistant manager if you were only an intern, or to position yourself as a team leader when you weren't.

You'll probably go along with their suggestions. After all, they're the experts. What do you know?

But you're stuck defending the claims you've made. If they're not accurate or are overstated in any way, or if one of your former employers contradicts your description of your title or responsibilities, you'll be the one left holding the bag. Too late to pin it on the resume designer. If you're caught—and the likelihood is you will be—you're basically screwed.

We have one sacrosanct rule for putting together a resume: *always tell the truth.* Do otherwise and it's the quickest way we know to, at minimum, lose the job you're after, and at worst, get yourself into serious hot water (think jail). How many cases do you know in which a falsified credential on a resume has surfaced twenty years later to ruin a prestigious career? It's in the media at least every week. And everyone who accesses that information ends up saying the same thing: "How could he [she] have been so stupid?"

Here are some other devices to stay away from:

CUTENESS

By "cuteness" we mean gimmicks. We think you should stay away from them at all costs. Employers hate them, they never work, and sometimes they can blow up in your face.

We once recruited a gentleman who was seeking a public relations position on the very visible "Got Milk?" American Dairy Association account. In advance of his interview, he thought it would be clever to send his resume and cover letter in a cardboard milk carton. Attention-getting, cute, creative—that is, until the hiring manager turned the carton over to get out the resume and sprayed herself with two-week-old sour milk. The candidate was right about one thing, though: she did remember his resume—right up until the time she threw it in the trash.

> **"CREATIVE" RESUMES DO MAKE YOU STAND OUT—IN A BAD WAY .**

Remember: cuteness kills.

LINES AND BORDERS

There's nothing wrong with using lines or even boxes on your resume, with one caveat: lines are okay if they make the resume more readable, or clearer; if they are for decoration only, leave them out.

COLOR

A resume is not a billboard to promote yourself. It is a business document, so treat it like one. Stay away from colored type, colored paper, colored borders, or any other gimmick to attract attention. Why? Because what you're attempting to do is completely transparent to hiring managers or H.R. execs. They feel they're being manipulated, and they don't like it.

PHOTOS

No, no, no! Unless you're looking for a job as an actor, don't let yourself get talked into including a personal photo with your resume. We know there are some "experts" who'll tell you it's a great way to personalize your resume and put a face on the cold, hard facts. It's not.

Think about it for a second. What's the motive for including a picture of yourself? If your resume is strong enough, an interested employer will arrange for a set of interviews, in which case there'll be ample opportunity to look at you. If they're not interested, your photo isn't going to change anything. One more thing: some companies won't accept photos with resumes; they fear being sued for discrimination.

VIDEO RESUMES

If you think we feel strongly about photos, ask us about video resumes. They're not new. They've been around since the nineties. And they never caught on because nobody, least of all a busy executive, wanted to spend the time sitting in front of a VCR watching an amateurish home movie. The practice showed promise of dying out.

Then came the CD revolution. Today, every employee has a computer on his or her desk. And every one of them has a built-in disc drive. Reenter the video resume, and with a vengeance. An article in the February 22, 2007, edition of *Time* magazine titled "It's a Wrap. You're Hired" commented on this increasingly popular phenomenon and suggested it could become the wave of the future. Even YouTube has jumped into the act. Many young people post their "resumes" on the site and direct their interviewers to a link.

But you're applying for a job now, not ten years down the road. Yes, there have been cases in which a given applicant was hired because of a video resume. But the practice is highly controversial, and will remain so as long as there's a multigenerational workplace. Don't forget, this is the first time in history when four distinct generations are represented in the workforce. Resumes get passed through a lot of hands at every level of corporate management. What might be seen as creative by a gen Y assistant product manager risks being viewed as sophomoric by a boomer executive vice president. (P.S.: Guess which person has more influence over your future with the company?) So before you start buying cameras, bugging your friends for help, and setting up a video production company, ask yourself if all the effort is really worth the risk.

Case in Point How badly can these video resumes blow up in your face? Consider the case of **Aleksey Vayner**. In 2006, Vayner, a student at Yale University, applied for a job with the investment banking firm UBS. His eleven-page application package included a seven-minute video clip titled "Impossible Is Nothing." This production, filmed to replicate a job interview, shows Vayner playing tennis (it's suggested he has a 140-mph serve), smashing a pile of bricks with his hand Jackie Chan–style, and bench-pressing weights (450 pounds). There's even a segment demonstrating Vayner's talent on the dance floor.

Instead of immediately being offered an interview, Vayner was dismayed to learn that UBS employees greeted the video with laughter and scorn. Under headings like "Too funny not to share," they e-mailed it to their colleagues and friends. In no time at all it was water cooler fodder at every major Wall Street firm. And like so many other embarrassing videos, it eventually found a worldwide audience on YouTube.

How would you feel if your video clip, designed to give you that extra edge in the employment selection process, became the overnight laughingstock of the industry in which you were seeking a job? Not too great, we'd guess. Did Vayner get the position? Of course not. Will he ever be given the chance to work at a leading New York investment firm in the future? It's anyone's guess. But smart money says his future job applications won't include a video resume.

We hope you've gathered by now that Hayden-Wilder is not a big fan of gimmicks or devices designed to attract attention. So what is the function of a properly prepared resume?

On the most basic level, a resume serves one purpose: to get you an interview. Crassly put, it's bait. If it's effective enough to motivate an employer to pick up the phone and schedule a meeting, it's doing its job. Conversely, resumes that don't make your phone ring aren't worth the paper they're printed on. Get rid of them.

What does it take to keep your resume out of the wastebasket and on top of the "set up interview" pile? Any effective resume needs to answer three questions: Why are you here? What qualities make you right for the job? What have you learned?

Most resumes we've seen don't even come close. They don't include a career objective or accomplishments, and often have only an abbreviated description of work experience. Tens of thousands of these "generic" resumes are sent out every year and disappear into a black hole, unseen, unread, and unanswered. Why? Because they make the employers work too hard to find what they're looking for. If a resume screener in H.R. is faced with sorting through a pile of two hundred resumes, he's not going to kill himself looking for the message that lies buried within. If you can't be bothered to properly showcase your credentials, why should he be bothered to dig for them?

IT'S YOUR STORY—TELL IT

How do you begin? At Hayden-Wilder we have a unique approach to resume development. We make a distinction between qualifications (what skills or experience you've acquired while going to school or working) and qualities (those aspects of your personality that add value to any task you take on). A major in accounting is a qualification. Ability to handle stress, or creative problem-solving, is a quality. In our book, the most effective resumes use the candidates' qualifications to showcase their qualities.

Here's what we mean. Let's say you played lacrosse at college. No big deal. Lots of students get involved with some type of sport. What's your first instinct? Put your athletic involvement as a line item at the bottom of the "Other Interests" section. Wrong.

Think about it. What does your athletic involvement say about who you are? Doesn't playing a sport talk to your taste for competition, your personal drive to excel, and your ability to effectively function as part of a team? We think so. Most importantly, don't you think a potential employer might care more about these aspects of your personality than your ability to handle a lacrosse stick?

Unfortunately, most resumes end up burying this information We think these qualities deserve to be highlighted, and we do it by giving them a preeminent position on the resume, one that can't be overlooked by even the most casual reader.

Hayden-Wilder has developed a unique resume format to showcase candidate qualities. It serves as a cornerstone for our entire Candidate Illumination program. There are five distinct sections: (1) the career objective; (2) business accomplishments; (3) work history; (4) education; (5) activities/skills/interests. Taken as a whole, they tell a compelling story about what makes the candidate unique and valuable to the potential employer. If you read one of our resumes, you'll know a lot more than the jobs the candidate held. You'll have a pretty clear idea of what the candidate is all about.

THE CAREER OBJECTIVE

This is the part of your resume in which you tell the reader why you're taking up his or her valuable time. In some ways it's the most important part of your story. Consider it your headline. Example: "*Career Objective:* A position in a global financial services company in which my research experience, education in world economics, and fluency in Mandarin would be considered valuable assets."

If your resume is being read by the right person, in one sentence you have gone a long way to assuring yourself a place in the "arrange interview" pile. Without reading your entire resume, an employer knows what industry you are interested in, your experience in research, your economics background, and your fluency in Mandarin. A pretty good start, don't you think?

Compare that with: "*Career Objective:* I would like a job in advertising because I'm good with people, am a hard worker, and want to learn." Or worse, a resume with no career objective at all. It may sound harsh, but companies don't believe you when you say you're a hard worker, nor do they care about your appetite to expand your personal knowledge base. They're concerned

> **YOUR CAREER OBJECTIVE IS THE MOST IMPORTANT PART OF YOUR STORY.**

with you using what you've learned to help them make money. That's why a good career objective focuses on what you can do for the company, not on what the company can do for you.

When do I need a new resume? One of the questions we're most frequently asked is, "Do I need a different career objective for each industry I'm pursuing?" In most instances, no. There's nothing wrong with expanding the industries mentioned in your objective as long as your skills and qualifications remain of value. Referring to the previous objective, it would be quite appropriate to say, "A position in a global financial services, research, or marketing company in which my ..." However, if you're looking for a job as a ski instructor, you're going to need a new resume.

BUSINESS ACCOMPLISHMENTS

To us, this is the most revealing part of your resume. It's not about the jobs you've held, or the tasks you performed while there. It's about a project you completed or a responsibility you assumed that demonstrates your suitability for the work you're seeking. Looking for a sales position? Find examples that demonstrate customer service skills, initiative, or strong follow-up. Want to get into management consulting? Think data analysis, research, and client service.

An effective "accomplishment" is a mini case history and will address these points: What was the existing situation or problem? What did you do to solve it? What was the result of your contribution? We generally encourage our clients to find three examples to cover the full range of work experience, staying away from those that are not current or that involve class assignments or projects. However, anything you've done on your own while at college is fair game. Maybe it was a fund drive you organized for a charity you supported.

Let's say you were applying for a space sales position at a monthly community magazine. The company was looking for candidates with strong customer service skills and sales experience. Which entry do you think would be more impressive to an H.R. exec looking for salespeople?

Inside Boston!

As part of an advertising sales team, was responsible for identifying and qualifying new advertisers for this travel and tourism publication. Analyzed advertisers in competitive publications, identified key contacts, and presold qualified companies for presentations by vice president of advertising. 2006 advertising increased significantly over the previous year.

> **Inside Boston!**
> - Advertising Intern
> - Competitive analysis, extensive new client research and outreach, developed support materials, maintained client databases
> - On-site sales of Boston visitor and restaurant guides

To us it's no contest. The first entry is much better.

We're sure that right about now you're thinking, "Are you crazy? What business accomplishments? I'm twenty-two years old, I have practically no experience, and my jobs were just dumb internships. What could I possibly say that would be of interest to an employer?" Well, guess what? We have never met a single client who, with a little prodding from us, couldn't come up with some pretty good business accomplishment case histories.

An example: Let's say you were waiting tables last summer on the Jersey shore. Nothing fancy. Worked hard, met some nice people, earned decent money. You think, not exactly a great resume-builder. But didn't you have to deal with difficult customers from time to time? You know the type. They complained the food was too cold or the service too slow. They had to wait too long to be seated. Every person who's waited tables has run into these situations. So how did you handle it? Did you throw them out of the restaurant? Or did the customer storm out the door, vowing never to return? We doubt it. Instead, you probably calmed them down, and by making them happy, kept them coming back.

You may not think so, but in our book, that's an accomplishment, and a pretty good one, too. What could be a better demonstration of your customer service skills than to defuse a difficult situation while retaining the customer? Any employer would be proud to hire someone with that degree of tact and people smarts. Our point is that even the most mundane summer jobs or internships can provide some very worthwhile accomplishments if you know where to look for them.

Congratulations! You're well on your way to creating a great resume. You've written a career objective clearly defining the type of job you're interested in pursuing. You've developed your extra-curricular experiences into a desired skill set. You've found two or three business accomplishments to demonstrate your attitude and ability. The toughest part is behind you.

At this point you should have filled about half a page. Most importantly, since we know that most employers don't spend more than thirty seconds reading a resume, almost everything you want him or her to know is right up front, where it will be seen.

WORK HISTORY

There's not much to say about this part of your resume. It's a chronological itemization of the jobs/internships you've held. Make sure you include the name of the company, the location (the city or town is sufficient), your position, the dates of your employment, and a *brief* description of your responsibilities.

BE PREPARED TO EXPLAIN ANY GAPS IN YOUR RESUME.

We've had a number of clients who left out work experience because they felt it wouldn't interest an employer. Wrong. Include everything. Even the most menial jobs, working in construction, waiting tables, being a counselor in a summer camp, all involve disciplines that interest hiring managers. They prove you can show up for work on time, deal with customers, handle money, work on a team. These are valuable assets. Don't bury them.

You may have taken a summer or two off—either to travel, go to summer school, or even to relax at home. If there are visible gaps in your employment history, be prepared to have an explanation for the interviewer. There's nothing wrong with taking a summer off. Just don't try to be evasive about it.

EDUCATION

This is very straightforward. The school you attended, its location, your degree, and any academic awards. One word of caution, though.

Your college's department of career counseling will urge you to put your education at the top of your resume. Why? Because every college thinks it is the most important thing about you. Perhaps it is, but

> **DESPITE WHAT CAREER SERVICES SAYS, DON'T LIST EDUCATION AT THE TOP OF YOUR RESUME.**

only to them. Put your education at the bottom of the page, where it belongs. An employer knows where to look for it.

ACTIVITIES/SKILLS/INTERESTS

This is the part of your resume where you let the reader know that you're more than a robot that does nothing but work and study. If you speak a foreign language or play an instrument, it belongs here. Are you familiar with job-specific software? Include it. Do you ski, have a pilot's license, love to cook? It all belongs in this section. But use common sense. Leave out the bungee-jumping and drag-racing— you can't really do your job if you're in a body cast.

One last thing: don't include your proficiency in the Microsoft Office suite, including Word, Excel, and PowerPoint. Almost every applicant knows how to use these tools. It won't buy you an edge, and it'll just take up space.

Look at the resumes on the following pages and see if they don't do everything you want a resume to do. They tell an employer the type of job you're seeking, highlight the personal qualities that will make you good at it, and provide the information needed regarding your work experience and education. Most importantly, they tell a story about you, a brand story that will set you apart from all the other candidates competing for the same job offer. And after all, isn't that what looking for a job is all about?

Mattie Whiteman Burke
76 Main Street • Boston, MA 02345
(617) 555-6787 • mattiewb@xyzmail.com

Career Objective

A Boston-area marketing communications or sales position in a tourism, sports, or life-sciences organization in which communications experience, strong writing skills, and lifelong personal interests in travel and holistic health are considered valuable assets.

Business Accomplishments

Inside Boston!, Boston, MA
As part of an advertising sales team, was responsible for identifying and qualifying new advertisers for this travel and tourism publication. Analyzed advertisers in competitive publications, identified key contacts, and presold qualified companies for presentations by vice president of advertising. 2006 advertising increased significantly over the previous year.

HealthWise Communications, Chicago, IL
Working on a team supporting the National Healthcare Workers (NHW), was given responsibility for writing announcement releases for newly awarded national contracts. With no prior category experience or knowledge, successfully authored healthcare releases, accompanied by newsletter articles. The releases were consistently picked up in both trade and business publications.

Walnut Street Gallery, Chicago, IL
Supported the opening of an upscale vintage clothing and art gallery, which had limited marketing resources. Wrote an announcement release, which was sent to local media outlets and national publications. Conducted media outreach to secure local coverage. The result: gallery traffic exceeded expectations, with several clients commenting on the media coverage they read.

Work History

2007 **Boston Sports Foundation**, Boston, MA
Development & Special Events Intern
• Responsible for solicitation and follow-up with donors for the major 2007 fund-raiser

2006 **Inside Boston!**, Boston, MA
Advertising Intern
• Competitive analysis, extensive new client research and outreach, developed support materials, maintained client databases
• On-site sales of Boston visitor publications and other guides

2006 **HealthWise Communications**, Chicago, IL
Public Relations/Marketing Intern
• Assisted in developing and executing communications plans, developed media lists, wrote press materials, media relations

2005 **Walnut Street Gallery**, Chicago, IL
Marketing Intern
• Wrote press materials and conducted media outreach, assisted in executing opening gala

Education

2007 **Boston College**, Chestnut Hill, MA
B.A., communications, *magna cum laude*

Activities/Skills/Interests

Conversational Spanish. Adobe Photoshop, Illustrator, Pagemaker. Varsity soccer, co-captain. Yoga Club, president. *Westwood Voice*, contributing editor. Tennis, homeopathy, reading, skiing, cooking.

Sierra C. Hunt
27 Elm Street, Birmingham, MI 11234
(313) 555-7890 • schunt08@xyzmail.com

Career Objective

A position in print, broadcast, or online journalism, in which writing proficiency, copy editing experience, and the ability to explain complex issues in concise language are considered valuable assets.

Business Accomplishments

University of Michigan Press, Ann Arbor, MI
As an acquisitions intern, was charged with managing illustrations and photos for inclusion in a new social commentary, Comedy and Politics. Successfully identified, researched, sourced, and negotiated pricing and usage. Delivered final recommendations for inclusion in a critically acclaimed "richly photographed" book.

Chicago Museum of Contemporary Art, Chicago, IL
Assigned sole responsibility for analyzing financial data and writing a grant proposal to renew Ford Motor Company's corporate funding for a lecture series aimed at young professionals. Completed the entire project in a two-week time period. The result: $100,000 Ford funding for the museum's "Art In the City" series.

Colorado Publishing, Denver, CO
Copyedited an anthology of 50 environmental advocacy speeches and song lyrics in *A Greener World*, by Abigail Rotheim, with a foreword by Al Gore. Prepared entire manuscript for printing, including checking documents for missing phrases/lyrics, fact checking biographical data, excising extraneous text, and insuring uniformity of editors' introductions. The book is cited by environmentalists as a definitive reference source.

Work History

2006-07 citysidewalks.com, New York, NY
Contributing Writer
• Authored articles on New York culture and social life

2005 Chicago Museum of Contemporary Art, Chicago, IL
Development Department Intern
• Wrote and edited grant applications, corporate fundraising materials

2003 University of Michigan Press, Ann Arbor, MI
Acquisitions Intern
• Managed research and correspondence to obtain illustrations and photographs for manuscripts

2002 Colorado Publishing, Denver, CO
Editorial Intern
• Assisted in collecting and editing documents to prepare manuscripts for publication

Education

2006 University of Michigan, Ann Arbor, MI — B.A., English & Journalism (double major)

2007 New York University, New York, NY — Graduate studies in Journalism

Activities/Skills/Interests

Copy Editor *Michigan Moments*: Edited news, arts editorial, and sports features for biweekly campus publication. Photo Editor *The Guild*: Literary Magazine. Fluent in Spanish. Sailing, scuba diving, tennis, film.

YES, THOSE LETTERS REALLY ARE IMPORTANT

So many of our clients struggle with the challenge of writing a cover letter or thank-you note. As we mentioned in chapter 8, writing skills in general have deteriorated over the years, and letter writing is a truly vanishing skill. There's no doubt that some of your apprehension could be due to the fact you've had very little opportunity to write letters. You're probably great at e-mails, text messaging, and IM-ing, but who writes letters anymore? Well, it's time to wake up. Letters, memos, and other forms of correspondence are regularly used methods of business communication. Now is the time to start honing those skills.

If you're like most of our clients, you probably look at thank-you notes as the painful price you pay for a nice birthday or holiday gift. If you lived in a household where you were expected to write them, we applaud your parents.

If you never had to send a thank-you note after being a guest for a weekend, or after receiving a lovely gift, we think your parents did you a great disservice. Thank-you notes are sure indicators of good manners; don't write them and you risk being seen as rude and poorly brought up. In other words, by ignoring this simple act, you have confirmed your status as a card-carrying member of the entitlement generation. You've got to change your evil ways.

We've spent a lot of time in our program working with clients to develop compelling cover letters and appropriate thank-you notes.

A SNEAK PEEK INTO YOUR PERSONALITY

A few months after launching Hayden-Wilder, we were interviewed for National Public Radio's popular show *Market Place*. Following the airing of the interview, the phone started to ring and our e-mail boxes pinged with new messages. There were inquiries from potential new clients. We immediately returned those calls! There were calls from financial planners who wanted to invest the vast (read zero) fortunes of our start-up company. We received calls, e-mails, and promotional materials from office equipment suppliers, phone service companies, computer experts, and many more. Although we returned every call and e-mail, we freely admit that we took our time. These types of inquiries were not important to us, but being polite communicators, we got back to everyone.

We also received inquiries from individuals who were interested in working for Hayden-Wilder as full-time employees. Interesting. We read these inquiries carefully and listened equally as intently to their voice mails. Why? Because we knew we could prove a point we often talked about with our clients: most of the correspondence and voice messages employers receive are either too long, too boring, too clipped, too vague, too jumbled, or too similar to every one else's messages. And then we received an e-mail that caught our attention more than any of the others we received. What do you think of it?

Dear D.A. and Michael,

I nearly dropped my coffee when I heard about your company in a WBUR [NPR] segment this morning. Any chance you're hiring, or may consider doing so in the near future?

My name is Kristen Stein, and I've been in brand planning for about ten years—primarily on youth-focused accounts—at agencies like Saatchi and Saatchi, Grey Worldwide, and AMP Insights (the research division of Alloy Media & Marketing). I am currently exploring opportunities that harness my experience but are not in a traditional agency environment, and it happens that recruiting and H.R.-type positions have been the focus of my search. It certainly seems that Hayden-Wilder would be a good fit given these objectives, plus I would love the chance to contribute to the growth of such a clever and timely concept.

My resume is attached and my mind is open. Any interest in meeting?

Best,
Kristen Stein

Finally, we had received an e-mail from someone who had cracked the code. This young woman captured our attention. We liked Kristen's e-mail because it was smart, to the point, conversational, full of energy, and flattered our business. She shared her qualifications with us without repeating her entire resume. Kristen received a prompt return call from us and we enjoyed a long phone conversation with her.

We weren't in a position to hire anyone so early in our company's existence, so we didn't schedule a meeting with Kristen. But if we had had an available employment opportunity, Kristen would certainly have been among the first people invited into our office.

We then proceeded to dredge through the other lengthy missives we received, many of which were complete with attachments worse than the cover letter itself. The letters we were receiving were exactly like those so many colleges encourage their recent graduates to write. Ugh. The letters were too long, boring, and stiff, and gave us no sense of what the candidate could do for us. They were generic and did not speak specifically to our business. They could've been sent to any other company without a single revision. (Even after one letter, our eyes were glazing over— imagine reading dozens of these drab missives. That is what hiring managers do.)

SHARE YOUR QUALIFICATIONS WITHOUT REPEATING YOUR ENTIRE RESUME.

In fact, many of the letters we received were amazingly similar to an example of a letter recommended by a liberal arts college in New England, which we use as a bad example to share with our clients. To show you what we mean, we lifted the following letter directly from a booklet provided by a college career services department. We've found these booklets are shared by universities throughout the country. The only difference from school to school is the name of the college on the front cover. (How generic can you get?) What do you think of this letter?

To Whom It May Concern:

I am very interested in applying for the Debt and Equity Markets Analyst position. I was made aware of this unique program by visiting your Web site and contacting your company directly in New York.

I am a senior at [XYZ] College and am interested in pursuing employment options with a prestigious investment banking firm like Sublime Stocks and Sons upon graduation. I will graduate with a Bachelor of Science degree in Business Administration with concentrated studies in Finance.

This exciting program will provide me with the necessary training and exposure to a wide variety of product groups. The Debt and Equity Markets Analyst position also allows me the opportunity to apply the knowledge that I have gained during relevant employment and coursework, especially my internships. Along with my internships at Fidelity Investments, I have also worked for Deutsche Bank in London, where I developed an appreciation for the fast-paced life on the trading floor. These experiences have enabled me to form a solid understanding of the financial markets and various computer programs relevant to the field. The analyst position in Debt and Equity Markets will offer me the opportunity to continue developing my analytical skills, while my goal-oriented attitude will enable me to make a strong contribution to your organization.

Enclosed is a copy of my resume. References are available upon request from the Career Services Center at [XYZ] College at (123) 555-7890. Or you may e-mail me directly and I would be happy to provide references from the aforementioned companies.

I hope you will call me in the near future to see if it would be possible to interview with the appropriate person at his or her convenience. Thank you for your time and consideration.

Sincerely,
Brian Smith

In comparing the two letters, we liked Kristen's e-mail because we could relate to it easily, having spent many years in the advertising business. Yes, her e-mail was pretty casual, but so is the ad biz. And with her ten years of experience, she could afford to be more relaxed in her writing style.

> **REMEMBER, EMPLOYERS HIRE PEOPLE, NOT FACTOIDS.**

If you think about it, the cover letter accompanying your resume provides the only opportunity you have to share a bit of your personality with the reader. Your resume covers your career objective; work history; education; and activities, skills, and interests. It's designed to be a factual document, with little room to share any personal information. Conversely, your cover letter can offer a little more insight into the actual person behind the facts. Remember, employers hire people, not factoids, so you can use your cover letter to your advantage.

CAPTURE ATTENTION WITH A MARKETING STRATEGY

When you read Kristen's letter, you probably recognize a few attention-getting qualities. Energy. Approachability. Humor. Smarts. The letter from Brian Smith featured in the college booklet shares none of these qualities, nor does it offer any personal insight about the candidate.

The other thing Kristen did to immediately excite us is found in the first sentence of her letter: *"I nearly dropped my coffee when I heard about your company in a WBUR segment this morning."* In this short sentence Kristen grabbed us because she had done more than the requisite research; she had actually heard us on the radio and shared a very favorable reaction to our business. This is an effective marketing strategy.

If you think of the first sentence in your cover letter as the place for your marketing strategy, you'll attract attention every time. The best marketing strategies are simple. If you are writing to someone at the recommendation of a friend or colleague, let the reader know it immediately. *"Neda Ahmed suggested I write to you regarding the opportunity to work for the* Chicago Tribune." If Neda Ahmed is someone the reader respects, you've grabbed his attention, and he'll continue reading your letter. Using the name of someone relevant to the reader is one of the smartest marketing strategies around.

Other strategies include:

- Sharing a personal experience you've had with the company or product. *"I've worn Adidas for years, and recently completed the Philiadelphia Marathon wearing your adiZero Pros. They are truly a runner's dream shoe."*

- Sharing an observation. *"As a resident of Los Angeles, I was fortunate to have been one of the attendees at the Green City conference your company hosted last week."*

- Sharing a recent news story. *"I've been following the Johnston Company since you relocated to Richmond and was very pleased to see the positive coverage you received in the* Post's *Sunday article about bioengineering."*

As you research and explore opportunities, it's important to include a marketing strategy in the first paragraph of your cover letter. Remember, you only have a moment in which to catch the reader's eye.

WHAT CAN YOU DO FOR THE COMPANY?

The second paragraph of a good cover letter should give the reader a taste of your experience and why it's relevant. This is *not* where you write about how you will benefit from employment at the company. Don't make the same mistake Brian made in his letter. At this stage of the game, the interviewer doesn't care about you. He wants to know how you can help his company. Pure and simple.

Use this paragraph to quickly highlight some of your experience, and connect it directly to the company. *"My internships with the*

Charlotte Hornets and the Portland Sea Dogs gave me hands-on experience and solidified my understanding of grassroots sports promotion and the importance of connecting with community con-stituents. I'm confident I could hit the ground running as a member of a team charged with developing community relations programs for the Milwaukee Bucks." That's all you need to do. There's abso-lutely no need to reiterate your resume. After all, it's attached to the cover letter.

TAKE CONTROL

We talk a lot about taking control throughout this book. Here's another way for you to take control of the search process and take the onus off the potential employer.

You've probably seen letters that end in a sentence that goes some-thing like this: *"I've enclosed a copy of my resume and I look forward to hearing from you."* Or, *"I've enclosed my resume for your review. Please call me at your earliest convenience to schedule an interview."* Or, *"I will expect to hear from you to discuss a convenient time for an interview."* All of these closing sentences put responsibility on the employer to call you. And guess what? Nine times out of ten employ-ers will abdicate that responsibility. They don't have the time to fol-low up on the flood of letters they receive, particularly those that don't relate to their immediate bottom line.

Instead, take control of the follow-up yourself. You achieve two things: (1) you create a legitimate reason to call the potential employer, and (2) you put the employer at ease knowing that she doesn't have to worry about one more thing to follow up on. Try a concluding para-graph like this one: *"I've enclosed a copy of my resume for your review. I will call you in a week in hopes of arranging a meeting."*

LETTERS THAT GENERATE RESULTS

There are two types of cover letters you'll be sending during your search process. The first is an invited/solicited letter. This is a letter you send in response to either a referral or an invitation to contact someone *("Joe Schmoe suggested I write to you")*. An invited/solicited letter is also used as a response to an opportunity you know exists *("I'm writing in response to your recent posting on my college career services Web site")*.

The second type of cover letter is uninvited/unsolicited. Think of these letters as written versions of cold calls. You'll write an uninvited/unsolicited letter to a company in which you have no personal contact. In these letters, the marketing strategy you use in your first paragraph is going to be particularly important.

Here are three examples of cover letters our clients have used to secure meetings. You'll see that the first letter is invited/solicited and the second and third are uninvited/unsolicited.

Dear Ms. Pingree:

When I saw your ad in the *Boston Globe* for a banquet manager, I was excited and delighted at having found not just an opportunity, but the opportunity to work in the professional, elegant atmosphere of the famed Ritz-Carlton. I bring three things to the party: six years of experience in catering and food service, a sophisticated education, and a real passion for the business.

I love working closely with clients to make sure their parties not only are successful but exceed their expectations and allow the host to enjoy the event just as much as the guest. I understand the demands and pressures of this business, have been tested and driven by them, and have consistently excelled and delivered.

I've enclosed a copy of my resume for your review and will call you in five days in the hopes of arranging a meeting.

Sincerely,
Brie Anne Williams

Dear Ms. Cranston:

As a recent [XYZ] College graduate with a love for interior design, but an extremely limited budget, I've fallen in love with the Home section of the *Washington Post*. As a member of the [XYZ] Alumni Careers Network, I know you're willing to speak to recent alumni looking to break into the field of journalism. I'm hoping to take you up on your kind offer of help and advice for a fledgling journalist.

I've been fortunate enough to have had wonderful internships at Basic Books, Yale University Press, and the Chicago Symphony Orchestra. I know the journalism skills I have acquired would be put to good use in the print or broadcast worlds.

I've attached a copy of my resume for your review. I'll call your office to follow up. Thanks in advance for your time and consideration.

Sincerely,
Margot Trabulsi

Dear Mr. Fells:

I'm writing to explore potential sales or customer service opportunities with Rossignol. After skiing everything from the Z9s to the B Squads at Jackson this winter, I found it easy to recommend your skis with confidence. I must tell you, Rossignol helped many of my customers enjoy great winters as well.

As an outdoor enthusiast and three-year employee of Teton Village Sports in Jackson Hole, I am well aware of Rossignol's dominant role in the ski industry. The company has distinguished itself through innovation, quality, and performance. The past three years in the outdoor industry have shown me that the ability to conduct business in this manner rarely goes unnoticed by customers and oftentimes leads to great success.

I've attached a copy of my resume for your review, and will contact you next week in hopes of arranging a meeting.

Sincerely,
Barret Joyce

All three candidates succeeded in finding great jobs. Brie Anne is a catering manager at a luxury resort in Florida. Margot is working as an assistant editor at a metro New York daily newspaper. Barret moved to Salt Lake City, where he is a sales manager for a major supplier of ski equipment.

WHAT WORKS?

As you compare the letters we've shared, here are some important points to keep in mind.

Keep it short and simple. If an employer spends at most thirty seconds with a resume upon first receipt, that same employer spends less time looking at the cover letter. As mentioned in the previous chapter, most of the employers, H.R. screeners, and executive assistants we know put incoming cover letters and resumes in three distinct piles:

- no/reject
- read
- might read if time allows

It's sad but true: the easiest way to separate correspondence into these stacks is to scan the length of the cover letters. If it were you, you'd do the same thing. You'd look at the short cover letters first; it's an easier read.

Please stop calling me "Madam." "Sir," "Madam," "Manager," "Dude," and, worst of all, "To Whom It May Concern" are all completely unacceptable. Be sure to use a real name and title, check them for accuracy, and spell names correctly.

Are you writing a mystery novel? Tell your reader what the letter is about right away. You have only a second to establish yourself. Don't expect the reader to pore through your letter to find out why you're writing. She won't do it.

Nobody likes a bragger. Stay away from writing about qualifications that can't be quantified. Eliminate sentences like *"I have great writing* skills . . ." or, *"I'm sure my vast experience and excellent people skills will be a great asset . . ."* Exaggerations rouse the "sounds suspicious" sense in readers.

Are you likable? Read your letter aloud before you send it. Do you have energy? Are you interesting and approachable? Or are you boring? (Would you ever use the word "aforementioned" in a conversation?) If it's the latter, you need to start over.

Remember your reader. Don't waste a lot of time and words describing how you might benefit by joining a specific company. The employer doesn't care. Instead, explain how your current relevant experience could immediately help move the employer's business agenda forward.

Check and source your facts. Rather than writing *"I read an article in the newspaper that sparked my interest in your company"* try, *"I read an article about your company in the June 30* New York Times.*"* You'll sound much more credible.

Don't forget to sell yourself. You are looking for a job, after all. Find the fine line between being an obnoxious braggart and a weenie. In the first paragraph, try complimenting the company or flattering the reader so he continues reading to learn more about you.

FIND THE SWEET SPOT BETWEEN BEING A "HOT DOG" AND A WEENIE.

DO I REALLY HAVE TO WRITE A THANK-YOU NOTE?

The simple answer is "absolutely." While a thank-you note won't win you the job, the lack of a thank-you note will definitely hurt your candidacy. We can't believe how many people don't write a thank-you note after an informational meeting or interview. Whether the meeting was a disaster or a smashing success, you must follow up with a thank-you. Most employers will look at a thank-you note as an example of good follow-up, a key to succeeding in any job.

At Hayden-Wilder, we often meet with individuals for informational or networking purposes. Both of us always comment on how a timely thank-you note prompts us to follow up on promises we may have made during the meeting. We're also snarky enough to comment negatively on those people we've never heard from again.

Be prompt. Your thank-you letters should be sent no later than twenty-four hours after your meeting. If you are interviewing with a very conservative company it is permissible to send an e-mail thank-you followed by a regular-mail copy. It's perfectly okay to send a thank-you at the end of the day of your meeting. And it's also all right to send an e-mail thank-you after business hours. Lots of people get caught up on their correspondence after 6:00 P.M. A prompt thank-you proves you're on top of your game. But don't send a note within two hours of your meeting—you'll get a cool reception, and the recipient will think you didn't put any thought into the note. We recently met a corporate recruiter who was interviewing students at Harvard University. The recruiter complained about how fast he was receiving thank-you notes from candidates. He had completed an interview and thirty minutes later was already receiving a thank-you note on his BlackBerry. This particular e-mail message had been sent with "urgency" and interrupted his attention from another Harvard candidate he was interviewing. The recruiter's reaction was, "That's just ridiculous." We completely agree.

Thank everyone you meet. If you met with four people at the company, be sure to send thank-yous to them all. We realize you may know that only one person can offer you a job. But never forget that the other three can greatly influence the decision-maker. That's why they *all* met with you in the first place.

Be accurate. The best source of information for titles and company/division names is a business card. Be sure to get a card from everyone you meet. Check and double-check to be sure you have the details correct. Watch out for division vs. corporate, U.S. vs. International, Inc.s, Co.s, d.b.a.s, and LLCs. These may seem like little details to you, but they're big deals to the recipient of your letter.

Keep your content concise. Just like a cover letter, brevity is appreciated in a thank-you note. Be sure to include these key pieces of information:

- Thank the reader for his or her time, and include the date of the meeting.

- Reference something that interested you in the conversation, even if you were bored to death.

- Sell yourself by quickly recapping why you'd be great for the job.

- Include any information you may have promised (an article, a link to a Web site, etc.).

- Take control of follow-up steps and recap what is expected to happen (are you supposed to call, or is the interviewer supposed to call you?).

Your thank-you note should be something like the one on the following page.

DON'T REINVENT THE WHEEL

Here's the good news about cover letters and thank-you notes. You don't have to feel as though you are sitting down to a blank screen every time you write. Despite what you think, the purpose of writing a cover letter is not to inflict tremendous self-torture. Once you've nailed a good second and third paragraph of a cover letter, the only thing you'll need to change is the first paragraph, with your marketing strategy—and that's only two sentences. You can handle it.

The same holds true for thank-you notes. Once you have a good template in place, you can use it over and over. The only part you'll need to tailor is the first two sentences. See, it's not so bad after all.

> **ONCE YOU HAVE A GOOD TEMPLATE IN PLACE, YOU CAN USE IT OVER AND OVER AGAIN.**

Dear Mr. Wienblatt:

Many thanks for meeting with me yesterday morning regarding the IT assistant position.

I thoroughly enjoyed learning more about [XYZ] Company and was particularly interested in the information you shared regarding plans for technology outsourcing.

I'm confident that my experience, my tremendous respect for [XYZ] Company, and my enthusiasm for the position could make me a great fit.

As discussed, I look forward to hearing from you next week. In the interim, here's the link to the technology article I mentioned: www.abcd.com.

Again, many thanks for your time.

Sincerely,
Rashid Maling

SIX DEGREES OF KEVIN BACON

In 1994, three students—Mike Ginelli, Craig Fass, and Brian Turtle—at Albright College in Reading, Pennsylvania, invented the trivia game Six Degrees of Kevin Bacon. They based the game on a Kevin Bacon interview featured in *Premiere* magazine after the release of the movie *The River Wild*. In the interview, Bacon said he had worked with everyone in Hollywood, or someone who's worked with them. Bacon essentially positioned himself as the oracle of the Hollywood universe.

The premise of the Six Degrees of Kevin Bacon game is simple. Gather a group of people together. Simply name a movie star from any time in history and see how quickly you can connect the chosen actor, within a maximum of six links, to Kevin Bacon. Here are two quick examples commonly cited on the Internet:

Try connecting Paul Newman. Newman was in *The Color of Money* with Tom Cruise. Cruise was in *A Few Good Men* with Kevin Bacon.

Or try connecting Carrie Fisher. Fisher was in *Star Wars* with Harrison Ford. Ford was in *The Fugitive* with Tommy Lee Jones. Jones was in *Batman Forever* with Val Kilmer. Kilmer was in *Heat* with Robert De Niro. De Niro was in *Sleepers* with Kevin Bacon. That's five links, one short of the maximum allowed.

By the late 1990s, the parlor game had swept across college campuses around the country and had a huge Internet following. Six Degrees of Kevin Bacon then became a successful board game and book. In an interview with Jon Stewart, Brian Turtle recalled the invention of the game while he was in college, "It became one of our stupid party tricks, I guess. People would throw names at us and we'd connect them to Kevin Bacon."

Stupid party trick? Maybe. The perfect example of how networking works? Absolutely.

> **WE KNOW YOU HATE TO NETWORK.**
> **DO IT ANYWAY.**

THE POWER OF NETWORKING

Eighty-five percent of all jobs are awarded because of some personal contact (think "link") within the hiring company. Why? Because there is no better referral than a personal one. And, who better to trust when recommending a new employee than a respected employee already working at the hiring company? If you had to choose

> **85 PERCENT OF PEOPLE WIN THEIR JOBS THROUGH CONNECTIONS FROM AN ACQUAINTANCE.**

between two candidates who had exactly the same qualifications and background, what would be a strong way to break the tie? If one of those candidates had a recommendation from an employee or coworker, who could vouch for the candidate's character or work ethic, your decision would be made much easier. Why risk taking a chance on an unknown?

Human resource professionals know the power of internal recommendations. Many companies have referral programs in place as part of their employee benefits package. For example, look at the Web site for Racepoint Group, a global public relations agency with expertise in digital media relations. On the careers page, in the description of employee benefits, you'll find an "employee referral program" listed in the savings plans section. Typically, most corporate referral programs are paid based on the level of the person being referred and hired. Someone referring an entry-level employee could make $500. Likewise, a senior-level referral could yield the referring employee as much as $5,000. We've seen corporate referral programs successfully recruit employees in industries including financial services, automotive, technology, health care, media, and many more.

IT'S JUST TALK

Networking is, by far, perceived as the most daunting task recent grads face. Initially, our clients think networking means asking family friends for a job. They think they couldn't possibly build a network

> **IF NO ONE KNOWS YOU'RE LOOKING FOR A JOB, YOU MIGHT AS WELL TAKE A NAP.**

because they don't know anyone who could help them. They think they are too young to know anyone who is powerful in business. They think they are pursuing a career path that differs from everyone else's career and expertise. The bottom line: they are terrified to begin the process. No wonder, these perceptions of networking are absolutely outdated and flat wrong.

The objective of networking is to:

- share your brand story
- meet people who can help you in your search process

Networking, in its most basic definition, is simply talking to someone. And that's something we all know how to do. Why is talking to someone so important? Because you have a great brand story and need to get the message out. If no one knows you are ready, willing, and able to work, you might as well take a nap. You can't make people care about something they don't know anything about.

Networking is going to be the way you share your brand story and consistently deliver the message you have worked hard to develop. By sharing your brand story through a well-designed networking effort, you are gaining visibility where and when you need it most. It's time to advertise your personal brand. And your choice of media is not magazines or television, it's networking.

YOUR DATABASE: A LIVING, BREATHING ORGANISM

The first step in networking is to build a database of all the people you want to include in your network. Just like any other database you've dealt with, the key to a great networking database is dependent on two key things: accuracy and up-to-date information. Think of treating your networking database as a living, breathing organism. It needs constant feeding and attention.

It doesn't matter what format you use. If you're great with Excel, use it. If you prefer Word, use it. If you must have everything written down in a three-ring binder, so be it. You may want to try the ACT! contact database program. Just be sure you have all your information in one place, in one format, that's easy for you to access.

INFORMATION IS POWER

We believe that a great contact database should have sixteen cells for each entry, to include everything you need to know about your networking contact. If you have this information at hand, you are taking another key step in controlling your search process. You'll never have to guess about the person you are going to talk to. The sixteen cells are the following:

1. Contact name.
2. Title.
3. Company.
4. Assistant.
5. Company address.
6. Home address (if applicable).
7. Phone number.
8. E-mail address.
9. How I know this person.
10. How will I meet this person?
11. Date of first contact.
12. Method of contact (phone, snail-mail letter, e-mail). Attach copy.
13. Date of first meeting.
14. Topics covered.
15. Follow-up required.
16. New contacts acquired.

Seems like a ton of information, but it's all worthwhile.

Be sure you are accurate in completing each item. It could cost you in the long run. Although most corporate Web sites try to keep as up-to-date as possible, we never trust the titles they attribute to employees because this information can change in a second. Don't be lazy and accept everything the Web site says. Call the company to check on the person's title. If they give you a hard time and won't tell you what you want to know, get creative.

Assistants are the key to the mint when you are trying to reach busy executives. It's important to include information about the assistant in your database because this is one person who can easily bar your access to the person you want to meet. Befriend the assistant, be sure you address him or her by name, and be upbeat in your conversation. You may be thinking it's a pain in the butt to kiss up to the assistant, but here's what's happening behind the scenes at the office: at the end of the day, executives who have personal administrative assistants will spend between five and thirty minutes with the assistant to recap the day's activities and plan the next day. During this meeting, the boss will ask if there is anything else she should know about. In which scenario would you prefer to be the candidate?

Scenario one:

Boss: "Anything else going on?"

Assistant: "There's a guy, Bruce Davis, who has sent in his resume and called several times. He seems like a really nice guy. He's asking for an informational meeting. What do you want me to do?"

Boss: "You like him?"

Assistant: "Yes, I think you should see him."

Boss: "Okay. Book him in."

Scenario two:

Boss: "Anything else going on?"

Assistant: "There's a guy, Bruce Davis, who has sent in his resume and called several times. He's pretty arrogant on the phone and is a pain in the ass. He wants an informational meeting. What do you want me to do?"

Boss: "Get rid of him."

In the second scenario, Bruce was quickly dismissed and probably never understood why.

THE DEPARTMENT OF REDUNDANCY DEPARTMENT

Other parts of the database, which are extremely important to keep updating, are included in cells nine through sixteen. This is the sort of information you will really need to keep track of, particularly as you start to meet more people. No matter how sharp you are, after meeting twenty people, it's impossible to remember what you talked to each one of them about, so use your database to keep notes. It's embarrassing to have a second conversation with someone and repeat everything you talked about in round one. The person you are talking to will have one takeaway: *"This guy is on autopilot and has nothing substantive to say. He told me the same thing the last time I saw him."*

Follow-up with your networking contacts is *mandatory*. There are no two ways about it. Thank-you notes following informational meetings must go out within twenty-four hours. And if you talked about something you found interesting, let the networking contact know. He'll remember you much better.

 We had a client, **Emily Trulli**, who wanted to get into the hotel catering business. Each time Emily had a networking meeting with someone, the conversation always turned to food. Based on her newfound knowledge of the type of food the contact liked, Emily developed a terrific follow-up tool. She would include a link to a new, cool restaurant she thought would appeal to the person she had met, as part of her follow-up note. It worked wonderfully. Emily was favorably remembered by everyone she met. Her networking contacts introduced her to many more people. Emily eventually landed a job in catering sales with a five-star hotel.

YOU KNOW MORE PEOPLE THAN YOU THINK

You've put together your database format and bought into the idea of actually getting out there and meeting people. You have a great brand story to share and a great resume to leave behind. You're probably asking, "Who the hell do I put on my list?" It's amazing how many people you already know who can become networking contacts for you.

TAKE CONTROL AND MAKE YOUR PARENTS ACCOUNTABLE TO YOU FOR A CHANGE.

Now is the time to get your parents constructively involved in your job search. Don't just ask your parents, on the fly, who they know. Instead, arrange a formal meeting with your parents. Let them know how serious you are about networking. Take *control* and make your parents accountable to *you* for a change. Think about and talk with the following people:

Immediate and extended family members. Your parents, sisters, brothers, their in-laws, aunts, uncles, grandparents, and cousins are all useful resources. Many of these people are in relevant professional situations, or know people who are. Your relatives may be members of business or charitable boards, or belong to clubs and professional organizations. It's amazing how many people they know. Ask them who their friends are, about their businesses, and about their business colleagues.

The key here is to meet with each relative on a one-on-one basis. A group discussion around the Thanksgiving dinner table usually yields little or no concrete next steps. Instead, use the family gathering to either talk individually with Uncle David, or as an opportunity to schedule a meeting a few days later.

Fellow graduates and their parents. If your friends from college have already landed a job, talk to them and see what the company they're working for is all about. Even if it is not in the business you're focusing on, these friends have gone through the job search process and may have some people for you to meet. It's also very likely that a friend may have a boss who is willing to meet with you for an informational meeting and network you to some of his or her contacts.

Don't dismiss this opportunity. Throughout our careers, we have met with many friends of our entry-level employees. We were always happy to do so, and continue to meet with many nonclient entry-level candidates each year. Often, we were in a position to move an employee's friend in the direction they were interested in. Remember, even though your friend's boss is in the advertising business, he may know people in publishing, construction management, or a variety of other businesses.

We've had clients resist the idea of meeting with their friends and their friends' bosses. They feel inadequate, or as if they are competing with their friends. After all, you might not have a job and three of your friends already do. You might feel uncomfortable talking to your employed friends about your search. Our response to this apprehension is: snap out of it! You are talking to a friend. He may or may not be able to help.

YOU ALREADY HAVE AN EXTENSIVE NETWORK— TAKE ADVANTAGE OF IT.

It's that simple. Why have a friend at all if you can't ask for advice once in a while? And all you're asking of his boss is a quick meeting and more advice. There's no harm in that.

Think also about your friends' parents. What do they do? Who might they know? If you're looking to get into the field of environmental "green" development, and you have a friend whose mother is an environmental attorney, set up a meeting.

Faculty members and coaches. We know, not all faculty members are helpful. Nor is every member of the team going to capture the full attention of the coach. There are, however, many faculty members and coaches who can be tremendously helpful as you begin to network. If you had a professor you really respected or connected with, arrange a meeting. The same goes for coaches.

Remember, teachers and coaches meet thousands of people throughout their careers and may be in a position to suggest worthwhile people for you to meet. Don't expect all of your professors and coaches to help out. Focus on the one or two you really respect. Our client James Fogherty received a master's degree in advertising from a major New England university. He thoroughly enjoyed one professor, who taught account planning. It turned out that James's professor had a previous career in advertising research—exactly the field James wanted to pursue. James arranged a networking meeting with his professor and received lots of good advice and a few names to contact. The people James's professor suggested met with him and linked him to other research professionals. James is now working in New York as a director of research for an international direct marketing company.

> **UTILIZE YOUR COLLEGE ALUMNI DATABASE TO MAKE VALUABLE CONTACTS.**

Alumni. Your university's alumni are a tremendous resource for networking. Depending on the college, either the office of career services or the alumni/development department is the best resource to find alumni with whom to network. Most schools provide undergrads with access to an alumni database. The sophistication of these databases varies from college to college. We've worked with clients whose alma mater provides alumni names flagged by profession. We've also seen databases that highlight those alums who are regularly willing to meet with grads. And we've seen databases that list alumni by city and state, which makes the networking identification process a bit more difficult.

A word of caution: some universities limit graduate access to their alumni database. Check with your college to see how long you will be able to reference the alumni database. Be sure you will not be cut off six or eight months following your graduation.

Our clients have had great success networking with alumni. Most of the alums you contact will be interested in your background, what's happening on campus, and what you're looking to achieve in your job search. So be sure to do your homework. If you notice that the alum you're meeting with played lacrosse, research a few nuggets about the lacrosse team you can share in your meeting.

Yahoo! has launched a new site for alumni networking called Kickstart. As the site grows and signs on more companies and colleges, Kickstart may provide a good supplemental alumni networking resource. Check it out.

Family friends and professional acquaintances. These are all the people your family members interact with daily. Doctors, dentists, lawyers, caregivers, financial planners, yoga instructors, and more fit in this group. All of these professionals have client bases. As a group, family friends and professional acquaintances may touch as many as ten thousand people. This group constitutes a networking gold mine.

Case in Point → Our client **Leah Schwartz** graduated with a B.A. in psychology and a minor in creative writing from a small college in Oregon. Leah wanted to merge her skill sets and land a development job in a not-for-profit organization focusing on children. Leah met with her family attorney, who connected her with one of his clients who was an active volunteer in a local children's charity. Leah fell in love with the charity and was determined to find a way in. She then met with her family dentist and shared her dream job goal with her. The family dentist had a local television anchor as a patient. The anchor was the spokesperson for the charity Leah wanted to work for. At her dentist's suggestion, Leah called the anchor and arranged a networking meeting. After impressing the television anchor, Leah was introduced to the director of development at her target charity. Leah is now working there as a development coordinator and loving every minute of it. It took only four links in the Six Degrees of Kevin Bacon game.

Former employers and their associates. Now you know why it's important to do well in your summer jobs and internships, and why it's important to stay in touch, or at least leave a good lasting impression, with your former employers. It's time to call on them for help in your job search.

Maybe the maître d' or the wine steward at the ritzy restaurant where you were a waitress last summer isn't high on your networking list. We think he should be. Remember, networking is all about broadcasting your brand story. You know that the person greeting guests at the front of an upscale restaurant knows his customer base and knows what they do for a living. He could end up being a help to you.

If you succeeded in an internship, you had an opportunity to meet many people in the corporation and impress your boss. Don't hesitate to use these contacts in your networking effort, even if the internship was not in a field you are pursuing.

Colleagues and clients from previous jobs. When you think about the people you met in former jobs, think beyond your immediate boss. Think about the company's clients and your colleagues as well. If you worked at a golf club as a caddie, your manager may not be as significant a networking contact as some of the clients for whom you caddied. Likewise, stay in touch with your colleagues from previous jobs. They may now be working for an organization that interests you. As your former colleagues move around in jobs, more opportunities for you may surface.

> YOUR FORMER BOSSES AREN'T THE ONLY ONES WITH CONTACTS. APPROACH FORMER CLIENTS AND CUSTOMERS AS WELL.

Religious and professional organizations. This is an area that may or may not work for you. We've had clients who have benefited greatly by networking within major Christian churches in the South and the Midwest. We've also had clients whose parents were very involved in their local synagogue. Meetings with church leaders and rabbis often produce great names for networking your way into a job opportunity. Think of church leaders as you would family professional acquaintances. They know lots of people, all of whom are involved in different fields of work.

Community and political groups. Several of our clients have worked as interns for state and federal congressman, senators, and other public servants. Others have volunteered for political campaigns or in major efforts to benefit a community cause (building a new school, protecting the environment, etc.). Our clients often overlook the networking contacts these positions provide, particularly if they weren't paid for the work they did.

Think about what you've been involved in and whom you've met. If you participated in a Habitat for Humanity effort, were there adults involved? Did you make a connection? If you worked on a political campaign, where did the other volunteers work? Usually, people who volunteer are well tied into the community and know lots of other people. By networking with these folks, you just may find the lead you need to land a desirable job.

Case in Point Our client **Paolo Estes** graduated with a B.A. in anthropology and a minor in sociology from a small liberal arts college in Minnesota. He wanted to work in state or federal government, in a research capacity. During the fall semester of his senior year, Paolo volunteered for the campaign of his local congressman, who was running for reelection. While working on the campaign, Paolo met a lobbyist who specialized in energy issues (not an area of interest for Paolo). Upon graduation, Paolo wisely contacted the lobbyist, who connected him with a variety of other lobbyists and related colleagues. As a result of his networking efforts, Paolo identified and landed a job with a political research firm, as a field researcher. It wasn't the government job he dreamed of, but he understands that his job in field research will provide him with valuable qualifications he'll need to make the switch to a government position.

FOCUS ON FIVE COMPANIES

In our experience, job banks aren't a particularly effective method to use to find jobs, and we believe applying for a job through a job bank is probably the least productive way to land a job. Conventional wisdom tells us that the majority of available positions aren't advertised.

That's why networking is so important. Job banks can be, however, a very useful tool in identifying and targeting companies that may be hiring. Monster and CareerBuilder, among others, are great sources of information on which companies are growing, and what areas in the company are experiencing that growth.

In chapter 12 we talk about researching target companies prior to an interview. The same holds true with networking. Put together a list of five companies you'd really like to work for. Then begin to research these companies, using conventional tools and job boards. Try to find out not only about the company, but also about its people. Use the Six Degrees of Kevin Bacon game and challenge yourself to find out how you might be able to network your way into the company.

Case in Point Our client **MiLin Kwan**, an art history major, came to us with a long-term goal of becoming a museum curator. MiLin was very shy, and resorted to job databases to make all her connections. For five months, MiLin applied for jobs online. She received minimal to no interest and a few flat-out rejections.

What MiLin had neglected to do was to find a more relevant way of *connecting* with museums, galleries, and other art venues. After meeting with Hayden-Wilder, MiLin identified her top five art venues. She then conducted extensive online research to see if there were people involved with each venue whom she could network her way in to meet. Bingo. It turned out that the husband of one of MiLin's art history professors was on the board of a well-known artists' cooperative. MiLin met with him, and he suggested she meet several other people he knew in the art world. Through her networking, MiLin eventually landed a great entry-level job with a city museum; the job was created just for her. She is now an assistant curator. MiLin would never have found out about the job online.

MAKING THE NETWORK WORK FOR YOU

Let's say you've done a great job networking and now have about sixty contacts in your database. How can you manage them all and differentiate the important from the less important contacts? Does every contact have the same amount of importance? If so, whom should you contact first?

There's no way you can contact all sixty people at the same time and maintain any sense of order and accuracy in your database; it's too overwhelming. Hayden-Wilder has developed a simple priority rating system to help make your database increasingly more functional. Our system ranks networking contacts, in decreasing order of importance, with number 1 being the most important.

Here's how it works:

1. Any contact employed by a company you want to work for

2. Anyone in the same industry, but not necessarily in a company you want to work for

3. Anyone associated with the industry you are targeting (e.g., lawyers, etc.)

4. Anyone generally well connected (an influencer/player)

5. Everyone else

If you rate the contacts in your database, you'll be able to quickly identify the people who are most valuable to you.

MIND YOUR MANNERS

It's important to remember that no matter how well you may know a particular contact, you are asking someone a favor when you set up a networking meeting. Respect that your contacts are interrupting their day to make time for you. Treat them accordingly. Prepare yourself before each meeting. Be professional, and be sure you reflect well on the contact by treating each informational/networking meeting as you would a job interview. Dress appropriately, even if you are meeting a neighbor in their backyard to network over a cup of coffee. Keep in mind:

Show you care. Try to remember pertinent personal information about each contact. Think about how you met the contact, what you have in common, who his or her friends are. Keep this information in your database.

Conduct research. Find out everything you can about the person you are meeting with, even if you think you know her really well. Google like crazy. Ask other people who may know the contact. The more you know, the more you'll avoid problems. We know one candidate who said great things about the chairman of a company, not knowing the chairman had fired her contact several years ago!

Practice. Be sure you are completely comfortable with your brand story. Write out the questions you have prior to the meeting and bring them with you. Present your thoughts in an orderly fashion.

Use your brand story. It will launch you into the substantive portion of the meeting. But be sure to exchange pleasantries first, so you don't come across as a rehearsed robot.

Follow up with everyone you meet. It doesn't matter if you think you'll never run into them again. Remember the Six Degrees of Kevin Bacon? The last thing you want to have happen is this:

> *"Hey, Joe, did you meet with Shawn?"*
>
> *"I met with him and gave him a bunch of information and names but never heard from him again."*
>
> *"You're kidding. He landed a job at Provident because of one of your contacts."*
>
> *"That's the last time I do that kid a favor."*

Let's say you meet with a contact you received as a result of a networking meeting. It is incumbent on you to let the original contact know you followed through and that you care enough to keep everyone up-to-date on your search. Send an e-mail update to your original contact. For example:

Dear Mr. Smith,

Thanks again for suggesting I meet with Tony, Sam, and Deidre. I've had great meetings with Tony and Sam, who were both very helpful. I'm waiting to meet with Deidre when she returns from vacation. I'll keep you apprised as my job search continues.

Sincerely,
Tom Carusone

Keep building your network. Be sure to get *three* other names of new contacts before leaving a networking meeting. As hard as this sounds, it's not. Try asking, *"I so appreciate your time and advice. I know you know so many smart people. Are there other people you think I should meet as I continue my search?"*

Establish daily goals. Remember, you have to care for and feed your network database. Make your goals reasonable and manageable. It's better to have a goal of reaching out to three people per day rather than trying to commit to reaching fifteen in a week.

Be upbeat. Stay positive at all times, even if the contact is the most boring person you've ever met in your life.

If you do the following three things, you'll be well on your way to success:

- Build an effective network.
- Share your brand story with all network contacts.
- Grow your network each time you meet with a new contact.

Networking—and job hunting, for that matter—is all about the Six Degrees of Kevin Bacon.

12: THE SECRETS OF EFFECTIVE RESEARCH

ALL I NEED TO DO IS LOOK AT THE COMPANY WEB SITE, RIGHT?

If you chose number 5, stick a gold star on your forehead. Not only is poor preparation cited most often, it's also at the top of the job-killer leaderboard by a significant margin.

Think about it from the interviewer's standpoint. It's the end of a long day. He's seen twenty-three applicants. So many names, so many faces. Enter the final candidate for the day. Her resume looks great. Top honors at a good school. Relevant work experience. Proficiency in Italian. Varsity lacrosse. She just might be the one. He lobs her an easy opening question, expecting her to knock it out of the park.

"Tell me what you know about our company." Answer: "Well, to tell you the truth, I don't really know too much. I think you do a lot in pharmaceuticals. You know, drugs. But I'm not certain which ones. And I think I read somewhere that you are doing a lot of research in the medical area. That's about it, I guess."

We admit that this answer may be slightly exaggerated for demonstration purposes, but it doesn't stray too far from the truth. Give a prospective employer a response like the one above and the interview is over. You might just as well get up and walk out of the office. Your potential employer—or shall we say, ex–potential employer—isn't listening anymore. You're toast.

Any hiring manager or H.R. exec will forgive a little awkwardness during the interview process—a blown question here, a little fidgeting there. And as long as you don't have a ring in your nose or a tattoo on your lower lip, they can even overlook certain personal style issues. What they can't forgive is any demonstration of laziness or a lack of passion on your part when it comes to their company. In their mind, if you're not interested enough to learn about your potential future employer, how desirable a candidate could you be? And why would they consider employing you?

On the flip side, we've had a number of clients who've pulled a southbound interview out of the fire by demonstrating their knowledge of the company with which they were interviewing.

Case in Point **Loni Gotshall** graduated from a terrific West Coast college with a major in statistics and marketing. Her dream: to move to New York and land a job with one of the major direct marketing firms working with big national clients. Through smart networking she finally managed an interview with a senior product manager at one of the world's most prestigious online marketing companies. The chance of a lifetime. She flew into New York the night before, and left herself enough time to do a couple of dry runs to their offices just to be sure she wouldn't get lost. She was ready, and she was pumped.

On the day of the interview, everything went flawlessly. She was a polite ten minutes early, read a copy of the *New York Times* in the waiting room, and was shown into the interviewer's office on the dot of 10:00 A.M. So far, so good.

Only one problem. Three minutes into the interview she learned there was no job, only an informational meeting. She was crushed, but decided to tough it out and forge ahead as though it were a real interview. Smart move. As the meeting progressed, Loni used the opportunity to demonstrate how much she had learned about the company. She let them know that she had read their annual reports, reviewed the appropriate industry publications, and even found some stock analyst reviews of the company and the industry. She knew their major competitors and had an opinion about their relative positions in the marketplace. In short, she probably had better information about the company and the industry than her interviewer did. And she let it show.

The product manager was so impressed with her enthusiasm and drive that he asked her to come back the following day to meet with his department head. Two weeks later she was offered and accepted a position as an assistant researcher in the company's online media division. Think this is a Cinderella fairy tale? It's not; it happens all the time.

We're talking here about the power of research. Not the "visit the Web site" kind, but a smart, imaginative, and thorough investigation of the company—its goals, strengths, weaknesses, and market position. It's called doing your homework. Good research can get you the job you want. In the process, you could also stumble across some information that influences you not to pursue a job that could end up a bad fit. Either way you come out a winner.

So here's our little pep talk. We know that doing the right amount of research is hard work, but it is worth it. You've probably heard the expression "Looking for a job is a full-time job." Although that's not totally true, what is true is that doing solid, attention-getting research does take a lot of time. We have scores of clients who landed jobs by being diligent about research. They found a contact who knew the right person in a company, or they discovered something unique about the company. Whatever it was, research helped them win the job.

We believe that research is one of the most effective and underutilized tools in setting yourself apart from the pack. Why? Because most applicants do it so poorly. Remember, inadequate research is

INTERVIEWERS' MOST COMMON COMPLAINT: CANDIDATES' LACK OF KNOWLEDGE ABOUT THE COMPANY.

the number-one complaint hiring managers have about entry-level candidates. Secondly, with the right kind of research, you can speak volumes about your drive, initiative, and curiosity, and do it in a highly credible way.

RESEARCH STRATEGIES

The company Web site isn't enough. Want to watch an interviewer's eyes glaze over? Recite everything you've learned from the company's Web site. It's predictable, it's boring, and all it says about you is that you're satisfied doing the barest minimum in learning about the company.

When employers say they're dissatisfied by the quality of research done by entry-level job applicants, they're talking about the candidates who only visit the corporate Web sites. It doesn't matter if you've memorized every detail of the company's history, know each division or subsidiary, and can recite the corporate mission statement in your sleep. If it's apparent to your interviewer that your only source of input is the company site, you're done before you start.

A Web site may give you basic information, but it is nothing more than a corporate ad to portray the host company in the best possible light. It's used to win customers, influence shareholders, and attract new employees. What you read on a Web page is there because the company wants it there, not because it's necessarily accurate or true.

COMPANY WEB SITES ARE NOTORIOUSLY INACCURATE.

Corporate sites are notoriously inaccurate. A company might sell off an entire division, change CEOs, and shut down 30 percent of its plants on the East Coast, and it'd take three months to show up on the Web site. So don't assume that what you read is current and up-to-date.

Want a peek at a company's future? Read the chairman's letter. Every publicly held company produces an annual report. This is a legally certified document issued to shareholders regarding the company's financial performance over the previous fiscal year. That means that unlike Web sites, corporations are bound by the truth. It's the law.

Every annual report opens with the chairman's letter. This is the place where the boss takes all the credit for the things that have gone right in the past twelve months and passes on the blame for the things that have gone wrong. It's also where the CEO lays out plans for the coming year and provides a vision for the future. You can't find a better way to learn what's really going on inside a company. If the corporation's headed for the tank, or if it's growing like crazy, you'll read about it here.

The point is that annual reports contain a gold mine of information about the organization itself and the market in which it competes. Most corporate Web sites have their financial information available for download.

And one more thing. There's no sense in going to the trouble of doing all this digging if you don't find a way to let your interviewer know it. But be subtle about it. No need to bash them over the head with how thorough you've been. Just ease a reference or two into the conversation. "You know, when I was looking through your annual report your chairman talked about taking a more customer-centric focus in marketing your products. What does that mean for your particular division?" If you don't get serious brownie points for that one, you don't want to work there.

Take advantage of financial reporting services. Financial analysts are heavily invested in the future performance of any publicly traded company. Why? Because they make their livings and their reputations on their evaluation of the investment quality of a given company's stock. That's what makes their research and analysis so thorough. They care about issues like prospects for growth, management stability, market trends, and competitive pressures—anything that affects the future of a company. These reports are published and are available through stock brokerage firms or securities traders and offer some of the best intelligence about a company or market. There's only one catch: this analysis is rarely free and often sells at a hefty price tag so it can be tough to get your hands on it.

For a less expensive alternative, try one of the more consumer-friendly sites, like Dow Jones.com and Hoovers.com. They offer a wide variety of industry and company reports that can be purchased by subscription or a la carte. Of the two, we think Hoovers offers more innovative and insightful perspectives.

Get the lowdown on your interviewer. If a company has been written about or reported on, it's somewhere on the Internet. Do you need to learn about a particular industry or marketing trend? It's only a click or two away. But the Internet has another benefit, and not many job seekers take advantage of it. The Web is a fantastic source of information about people. We're not talking about Facebook or MySpace; we mean the Internet as a whole. Don't believe it? Google yourself and see what happens. Chances are you'll find yourself mentioned somewhere. Maybe it'll only be an announcement of your graduation from college, or your involvement in some civic project in your hometown, but the chances are pretty good you'll come across something about yourself.

It stands to reason, then, that if you can find yourself on the Internet, you can probably learn a lot about your interviewer as well. Has she recently been promoted? If so, from where? How long has she been with the company? Where did she work before? Is she quoted in corporate press releases or has she addressed industry groups? If so, what was said? Chances are, if your interviewer is a reasonably senior member of the organization, her name will be on the Internet.

> **WANT SOME USEFUL INSIGHT? TRY GOOGLING YOUR INTERVIEWER.**

When it comes time for your meeting, you may not be able to use everything you've learned, but if you can bring some of your knowledge about the interviewer's background into play, we promise that person is going to remember who you are. Something like "I read the speech you gave to the Indiana Coalition for Mothers against Candy Advertising Directed at Children, and I thought you made some really great points." Everyone's a sap for a little flattery once in a while.

Don't fill your head with junk. You have a lot to think about when you go on an interview. Do I have spinach in my teeth? Are my hands too sweaty? Will he give me one of those killer behavioral questions like "Tell me a time when you lied to your boss"? Do yourself a favor and don't do a lot of irrelevant research that'll be of no use to you or your interviewer. You don't need to know that the Singapore office fell short of its fourth-quarter sales goals because of an unusually long rainy season. It's not important and no one cares. You're not writing a business case history, you're going on an interview. So get rid of the useless stuff and concentrate on what you're likely to need.

Do a research plan. How do you know what you need to know? Make a plan. There are lots of ways to go about it. The one we like contains three levels of information: (1) what you must know; (2) what will make you look good if you know; (3) what will make you a star if you know.

What you must know. We define this as any information that will make you look foolish if you don't know it. Things like: What does the company make or do? How large is it? Where does it stand in its category? What is its positioning (e.g., biggest, cheapest, highest quality, best customer service)? What kind of advertising/marketing is it doing? Who's the chairman? What are the specifics of the job you're applying for? Don't ever walk into an interview unless you know this stuff cold.

What will make you look good if you know. We define this as the sort of information that demonstrates you've gone the extra mile to learn about the company. You're not required to know it, but it will reflect favorably on you if you do. Why? Because most of your competition won't have made the effort. Some examples: Do you know the major trends in the company's category? Is it gaining or losing share? What near-term challenges does it face? Who are its major competitors, and why? What is the chairman's vision for the future? What does Wall Street think about the company's prospects? What do you know about your interviewer's background? You may never get a chance to use all of what you've learned by doing this level of research, but if you can find a way to let your interviewer know you've done it, you'll have hit a home run.

What'll make you a star if you know. This sort of information has only one purpose: to impress your interviewer. It works because it showcases the personality attributes of the researcher more than the research itself. This type of information-gathering is designed to underscore qualities of yours that a company might find of value in a future employee: initiative, creativity, perseverance, and curiosity, to name just a few. Be innovative in your research approach, for instance, and you'll be viewed by your interviewer as a creative, outside-the-box thinker.

Do your own research. Let's say you are applying for a training position at a major national banking institution. You know at the outset that every candidate they've scheduled for a day of interviews is going to have credentials every bit as impressive as your own. So how do you make them remember you? Tell them something they don't know.

What if you made a point of visiting a number of that bank's branches in a variety of different neighborhoods? You'd get a pretty good snapshot of what the bank's like from a customer's point of view. Are there long lines? If so, do they open additional teller windows? Are the branches clean and professional-looking, or messy and disorganized? Are the employees friendly and helpful, or bored and disinterested?

> **GET OFF YOUR BUTT AND DO YOUR OWN RESEARCH—IT'LL IMPRESS YOUR INTERVIEWER.**

Next, cross the street and visit some of the competition's branches. Ask yourself how they compare. What do they do better? What do they do less well? How does their selling approach differ from that of the bank you'll be interviewing with?

Now that you've traipsed all over town and seen the inside of an endless parade of bank branches, you might think that the hard part is behind you. Wrong. The most difficult task lies ahead. Take what you've observed and come up with an opinion. If your interviewers don't ask you what you think—and they will—then don't be afraid to tell them. Remember, you're being considered for employment in part for your ability to gather data and make judgments. This is your first chance to showcase what you can do.

Put yourself in the interviewers' shoes. Appreciate that by the time they get to your appointment they may have listened to a seemingly endless stream of candidates, and they're all talking about the same things: their summer jobs, their internships, and their educational backgrounds. Death by dullness. Give them a day or two and they won't even remember the faces that go with the resumes, much less what was said in the interviews.

Then it's your turn. You walk in, sit down, and straightaway let your interviewers know you've spent the last three weeks visiting bank branches—both theirs and their competitors'. You let them know what you think about what you've seen. Maybe you even have some ideas about marketing to new customers.

All of a sudden, there's only one face the interviewers remember, and it's yours. Why? First, because you didn't just sit at your laptop and surf the Internet, like everybody else. You actually went out into the marketplace. A plus for initiative. Second, you offered some intelligent opinions about the bank's in-branch marketing as seen from the customer's point of view. A for brains. And third, you said something they hadn't heard a hundred times before. A for creativity. In our book, that's a pretty good report card.

Obviously, this strategy can't work in every situation. If you're looking for a job at General Electric, you're not going to fly around the world and visit all their plants and factories. But in those cases in which your target company sells through a retail channel or has its own proprietary outlets or branches, you have a great opportunity to get firsthand experience with the product and the marketing. If that kind of effort doesn't impress your interviewers, then forget about them. You can work for us.

We've said it before, but it's worth repeating. It's not what you learn about the company that's important, it's what you let your interviewer know you've learned. There's no sense in compiling stacks of information about a potential employer if you don't find creative ways to weave what you've learned into the conversation.

Let's say your interviewer opens your meeting with the following: "Tell me what you know about our company." You can parrot back basic information that anyone can find on the company's Web site. Or you can sprinkle your response with facts that are less available or less well known. A recent reference to an article or speech you may have read, a quote from the annual report, an industry white paper. Which approach do you think is most likely to impress? We'd hire the latter candidate every time.

Remember, if you think of research simply as a method of acquiring information in preparation for an upcoming interview, you're wasting half its potential. Make it your secret weapon. It's also one of the most creative ways we know to show your interviewer who you are and what kind of employee they'll get if they hire you.

WHAT DO YOU MEAN, I CAN'T WEAR MY NOSE RING?

"If I wear a suit, do I have to wear the jacket?"

"It's a creative job, so shouldn't I wear something creative?"

"I think it's a casual company, so I'm wearing jeans to the interview."

"I never wear socks; it takes too long to put them on."

"I'm getting my hair done just before the interview."

"It's a fashion magazine, so I'm wearing Fendi."

"How much gel should I put in my hair?"

"It doesn't matter what you wear if you're smart."

"It's a high-tech job, so I'm wearing black jeans and a black T-shirt, like Steve Jobs."

"Oh my God, I hate wearing panty hose."

We run into questions and statements like these from our clients daily. As crazy as it sounds, it can be completely nerve-racking to get dressed for an interview. It's even more scary if you have to interview at one company over several days. After all, how many interview outfits can you reasonably put together when you've spent the last four years wearing the college "uniform"?

Like it or not, the clothes you wear, combined with your personal comportment, have a tremendous influence on the interviewer. It's just like the impressions you have of celebrities, who may or may not be turned out appropriately. When Christina Applegate or Reese Witherspoon are dressed and made up for the camera, the world thinks they are doing just great. But when Lindsay Lohan or Kate Hudson get caught by the paparazzi, wearing no makeup, with tight sweats and messy hair, the world thinks they're having a hard time of it. Something must be wrong. Although it's an extreme example, employers think the same way. When a candidate is well put together and exhibits great manners and comportment, he is far more attractive than the candidate who appears rough around the edges and sloppily dressed, even if both candidates have exactly the same qualifications. There is no getting around it. Employers react to the way you look, so it's very important that you *control* each and every impression you make during the interview process.

Case in Point We recently met with partners in a big-city law firm. The attorneys told us about candidates they were interviewing from law schools, to fill coveted junior positions at the firm. They told us the story of one candidate, **Janet Weiss**, a young woman with a degree from an Ivy League law school. Janet had stupendous internship and clerking experience. Her resume and application were far superior to those of the other candidates the law firm was considering. The firm sent two partners, at two different times, to interview Janet at her law school. Both times, she appeared bright and confident. She nailed her interviews, and the partners

> **THERE'S NO GETTING AROUND IT: EMPLOYERS REACT TO THE WAY YOU LOOK.**

were impressed with her. The last step in the process was to have her come to the firm to meet with the hiring committee, comprised of five partners. Janet arrived a few minutes late. She then fielded questions from the hiring committee for two hours.

As is the tradition, the hiring committee met immediately after Janet left the interview, to discuss her candidacy. The partners agreed she answered the questions beautifully. They agreed she was supersmart. And then the discussion moved to her tardiness for the interview. The committee discussed the fact Janet looked a bit disheveled and windblown when she arrived. They also thought she looked even more disheveled throughout the interview, because she fiddled with her clothes and hair. The ultimate decision: Janet didn't get an offer. Why? Because the partners agreed they were uncomfortable with her appearance and deportment. Janet had only one shot to make a first impression on the committee, and she blew it. They decided she would not be someone they could put in front of the firm's clients. It didn't matter how smart Janet was.

WHY IS IT SO HARD TO FIGURE OUT WHAT TO WEAR?

Fifteen years ago, when the term "business casual" became popular, companies throughout the country wrestled with what that meant to their employees. At conservative companies like IBM it meant implementing "casual Fridays," allowing men to wear jackets and sport shirts with no ties once a week. At financial institutions it meant the same thing. At advertising agencies, publishing houses, consumer products companies, and the like, it meant an entirely new way of dressing for work. Some employees stuck with suits, shirts, and ties, while others ran completely amok. When business casual was adopted in the advertising world, we saw clothes on our employees we didn't want to know they had in their closets. It seemed anything and everything was okay, and all judgment went completely out the window.

As casual dress has permeated business environments in general, an accompanying code of casual dress conduct also has morphed into the mainstream. As you begin to

> **YOU WIN SOME, YOU LOSE SOME, SOME GET RAINED OUT, BUT YOU DRESS FOR THEM ALL**

interview and spend time at more and more companies, you'll see that each has its own way of dressing—from very formal to very casual, and everything in between. You'll also see that companies are beginning to move back to more formal attire. This is particularly true for companies in service industries, where customer/client contact is a regular occurrence.

It's important to realize it is not up to you to try to understand a specific corporate dress code when you are in the midst of the interview process.

> **THINK CONSERVATIVE WHEN IT COMES TO TIES.**

So, quit worrying about being overdressed. No one ever lost out on a job because he or she dressed too well for the interview.

KEEP IT NEAT AND SIMPLE

If you honestly think your clothing is absolutely *impeccable*, you probably look pretty good. Men should wear well-tailored, conservative, dark suits. Dress pants and a dark sport coat are fine for more casual industries. Be sure your shirt is starched, and avoid wearing dark-colored Regis Philbin–style fashions. Don't wear dress shirts with contrasting collars and cuffs. White, light blue, or subtle pinstriped shirts with button-down or spread collars are fine. Watch your cuffs to be sure the dry cleaner doesn't leave a crease in them. Cuffs should be ironed all around so they fit perfectly on your wrist. Avoid wearing French cuffs—they're for successful and wannabe successful investment bankers and hedge fund mangers, and you haven't achieved that status yet.

Think conservative when it comes to ties. Foulard, two- or three-colored stripes, or small pin-dot patterns are best. And be sure to wear dark socks and polished shoes. We had a client, Brian, who was a terrific dresser but insisted on never wearing socks. He told us, "It takes too long to put on socks. If I have to wear a tie, and tie a decent knot, there's no way I'll have time to put on socks." Finally, after several conversations, we talked Brian into wearing socks. It sounds silly, but he couldn't thank us enough after his first interview at a real estate investment company. Everyone Brian met was perfectly attired—complete with socks!

Likewise, one of our clients who was looking to get into the production business, resisted the idea of wearing a jacket when he went on interviews with film and television producers in New York. "I hate wearing a navy blue blazer; it's too preppy," he whined, but he broke down and wore one to his meetings. After interviewing, he e-mailed us, "I'm so glad I wore the blazer. You were absolutely right. I would have looked like a lowlife without it on. The guys I interviewed with were really slick."

Women should wear pantsuits or skirt suits, with a tailored shirt, blouse, or turtleneck. Depending on the type of company you are interviewing with, skirts and sweater sets, or pants with contrasting jackets, also are fine. Whatever you do, don't look dowdy, as if you've never dressed for work before! Have a little fun with your outfit. Choose something chic and elegant but not trendy. Wearing a suit with a conservative jacket and a skirt with a flounce or fun pleats is much better than looking like "a woman trying to look like a man" in a suit. Conservative scarves and jewelry are perfectly appropriate. If you have multiple ear piercings (or other piercings, for that matter), resist filling each hole with an earring. Two are plenty. If you wear rings or a bracelet and are tempted to fiddle with them when you interview, take them off.

In creative fields such as fashion, publishing, advertising, public relations, marketing, retail, merchandising, and media, female candidates are expected to know what the current fashion is. So it's okay to show a little flair. But be very careful not to go over the top. *Never* wear your skirt too short—it's the kiss of death. Super-short skirts make male interviewers extremely uncomfortable, even if they do like ogling your legs. Female interviewers, by and large, find short skirts a signal of a lack of judgment by the candidate.

> **WEARING YOUR SKIRT TOO SHORT IS THE KISS OF DEATH.**

Case in Point ➤ Our client **Lindsay Greenwood** is a smart young woman who graduated from an Ivy League college in the mid-Atlantic, with a comparative religion major and a minor in mathematics. Lindsay wanted to work in the fashion industry, either in sales or finance. Lindsay completed summer internships at Calvin Klein and Bloomingdale's and considered herself "very style-conscious and good with people." Despite our best advice, Lindsay wore short skirts, low-cut blouses, and designer heels to her interviews. She looked ready for a night of clubbing, but certainly not for a budget or sales meeting. Upon inviting Lindsay to a New York

> **IF YOU HAVE MULTIPLE PIERCINGS, RESIST FILLING EACH HOLE.**

fashion house for a second round of interviews, a very frank and honest H.R. recruiter gave Lindsay a serious heads-up. The recruiter told Lindsay she needed to tone down her clothes when she came to meet with management if she was expecting to be taken seriously. Wow! A slap in the face? No. Lindsay was shocked, but she listened to her inside tipster. She showed up for her management interviews in a fashion-forward pantsuit with a high-collared blouse. Lindsay nailed her interviews and landed the job. She later told us management thought she had "great style."

PLATFORMS? HEELS? SANDALS? WING TIPS?

Arrgh . . . as much as you hate to wear them, women must wear hose and closed-toe shoes. We know plenty of hiring managers who won't even consider a candidate who shows up with bare legs for an interview. Wait to get the job and check out what everyone else is wearing before you come to the office with bare legs. You'll be a lot more comfortable appropriately dressed than underdressed every time. There are *no* exceptions to this rule, but we've heard it all: "I can't wear hose with these shoes because my shoes are a little too big and they slide off." Our response: buy a pair of shoes that fit, or put pads in the shoes you have so they do fit. Or, "My legs are really tan, no one will notice." Our response: people notice tanned legs, that's why you get a tan in the first place; so they will definitely notice bare tanned legs.

MANY INTERVIEWERS LOOK AT SHOES FIRST.

Shoes, for men and women, must be polished and scuff-free. Scraped heels on ladies' pumps and worn-down heels on men's shoes are other signals of lack of attention to detail. It's amazing how many employers comment on shoes. We've heard, "Shoes tell me a lot about a person." And, "I can tell how aggressive a guy is by the type of shoes he wears." Or, "Did you see her Manolos?" So the word on shoes is: wear them, but don't let them distract from the reason you are interviewing.

GO EASY ON HAIR, JEWELRY, AND FRAGRANCES

Rule of thumb: unless you are interviewing at a fashion or beauty company and are wearing one of *their* fragrances, don't use a scent at all. This goes for women and, importantly, men. We had a client, Brent, who was a finance major and played Division I men's ice hockey at a well-known New England university. Brent came into his Hayden-Wilder sessions smelling like the fragrance department at Macy's. He didn't realize his cologne was so strong, as he'd been wearing it for years. All we could think of was, "Why is this strong, smart, athletic guy spritzing himself with this disgusting-smelling stuff?" The fragrance totally took focus away from Brent as a candidate. God forbid if his interviewer had any fragrance allergies.

Don't try out a new hairdo at an interview. At best, it's risky; at worst, disastrous. If you need a haircut or a new hairstyle, be sure you get it a few days prior to the interview and are completely comfortable with it. Hair-flipping, hair-fussing, hair-twisting (around a finger), or running your fingers through your hair are all unacceptable in an interview. It's distracting to the interviewer and indicates insecurity by the candidate. Even if you believe you have the best hair in the universe, *please* keep your hair away from your face. If you have long hair, bring a barrette or an elastic to the interview in case you need it. If you are a hair product junkie, be careful. Too much gel or hairspray can be a real distraction. Err on the side of conservativism. If you can see the product in your hair, it's probably too much. Also, keep your sunglasses off the top of your head, no matter how expensive they are; if you don't, you'll look obnoxiously cocky.

BAG IT

If the French and Italians are obsessed with shoes, Americans are obsessed with bags. Bags of every size—purses, satchels, backpacks, fanny packs, briefcases, portfolios, gym bags—are attached to American bodies wherever you look. In

ONLY MESSENGERS GET HIRED FOR WEARING BACKPACKS.

areas where driving a car (with ample storage space) is not the norm, and people are more dependent on mass transit, bags are getting bigger and bigger. This applies to men and women alike.

What is the appropriate bag for an interview? Something small and compact is preferred. For women, this means a leather purse and a small portfolio, or a neat, sleek leather bag that can hold both your purse and your portfolio. For men, a leather portfolio is perfect; just be sure any college logo or monogram is subtle. Backpacks are *not* appropriate for interviews.

EVERYONE IS WATCHING, AND EVERYONE HAS AN OPINION

During the interview process, you'll be visiting a variety of office environments: corporate office parks, small storefront offices, high-security skyscrapers, doorman buildings, open office spaces, lofts, and cubicle farms. The moment you walk into any of these buildings, you are onstage. Everyone—from the security guard in the lobby, to the receptionist in the waiting area, to the assistant who escorts you to your interview, to the employees you could potentially be working with—is actively forming an opinion of you. And you haven't answered even one interview question! So think of all those eyes watching you and follow these guidelines:

> **EVERYONE IS FORMING AN OPINION OF YOU— FROM THE SECURITY GUARD TO THE DOORMAN.**

Say "please" and "thank you" to everyone you meet. Manners can never be stressed enough. You're called the entitlement generation for many reasons. One is that you have a reputation for looking down on people you don't consider important, so take a new tack. Be nice to doormen, security guards, janitors, assistants, and receptionists. Say "please" and "thank you," and say them often. Smile and say "good morning" to everyone. The boss is gracious to every level of employee and will solicit opinions of you. "Hey, Joe, what did you think of that kid who signed in at three o'clock?"

Do arrive early.

Do bring something appropriate to read while you wait.

Do be courteous to the reception- ist, assistants, and anyone else you come in contact with.

Do practice sitting with your hands in your lap, without fidgeting.

Do wear panty hose (if you're female!).

Do wear scuff-free, shined shoes.

THE DO'S AND DON'TS OF INTERVIEW DECORUM

Don't worry about being over- dressed.

Don't change into your interview shoes in the lobby.

Don't wear too much jewelry, fragrance, or hair products.

Don't wear a tie with "personality."

Don't ever, ever, ever wear a short skirt or a low-cut blouse.

Don't bring your backpack.

Change your shoes outside, not in the lobby. Pounding the pavement is tough, particularly in city environments where you deal with long walks, subways, buses, and unanticipated rainstorms, so feel free to wear casual shoes when you're traveling between appointments. But change your shoes before entering the lobby of the building where you are interviewing. Use the coffee shop next door, or the awning of a building nearby, as your personal dressing room. And if you are planning on changing shoes, be sure to put your casual ones in your briefcase or bag, where no one can see them.

Don't touch up your makeup and hair in public. Use the ladies' room for this purpose. There's nothing worse than meeting a candidate in the reception area by interrupting her as she looks in the mirror to fix her lipstick. It's a good idea for men and women to use the restroom before the interview, so you can give yourself a quick once-over. Check your hair, check your makeup, check to see if your tie is straight. Check your teeth to be sure you're not storing part of your lunchtime tuna sandwich between your incisors. And please, check your breath—and fix it with a breath mint, not a stick of gum.

MAKE A GREAT IMPRESSION ON THE ASSISTANT

As you found out in chapter 11 on networking, administrative assistants hold the keys to the mint. They wield power you wish you had. Assistants are like air traffic controllers—they make sure their boss's schedule is kept up to date and flowing freely—and they can adjust course as needed. For example, if an assistant checks you out in the waiting room and sees you reading a Batman comic (this really happened), the boss will be duly informed. More simply said, if the assistant likes you, he or she is going to tell the boss. If the assistant doesn't like you, he or she will tell the boss—even louder.

Bosses and assistants have their own private codes and languages, which can work to your disadvantage. Imagine the assistant doesn't like the candidate and tells the boss just before the interview. A classic signal from the boss to the assistant would be to comment, at the beginning of the interview, that he might be interrupted by an emergency conference call. Conversely, the assistant, reading the boss's mind, will interrupt the interview for an unexpected phone call. The assistant then politely escorts the candidate out the door, and the candidate never hears from the company again. Unfortunately, the candidate has no idea what just happened.

R.E.S.P.E.C.T.

Security guards, doormen, receptionists, and assistants aren't the only ones who deserve your respect. Remember, you are a guest in a company when you are invited for an interview, so it's important to act like one.

Whether you are male or female, stand up when someone enters the room during your interview. It doesn't matter if the person is the janitor, a vendor, or the CEO. You show a sign of respect by standing up and acknowledging the person's presence. There is no need to introduce yourself; let the interviewer introduce you if he or she considers it appropriate. In most cases, the visitor will say "thank you" and ask you to please sit down. The visitor *and* the interviewer will remember you as being well mannered and respectful.

If you are offered an office tour, by all means accept. A tour can give you a better sense of the work environment and provide insight into the type of people who work in the company. But be careful; the tour is not really for you. Actually, you are being put on display to the office employees, so *control* their impressions. Smile, no matter how depressing the office environment might seem. Acknowledge that your tour guide is leaving office responsibilities and deadlines behind to squire you around. Ask questions and appear appreciative. If you are fortunate enough to meet some employees during the tour, be sure to be upbeat, enthusiastic, and interested in what everyone is doing.

SMILE, NO MATTER HOW TERRIFIED YOU ARE.

Case in Point We recently had a client, **Miriam Stokes**, who was clearly impacted by an office tour. Miriam had three interviews at a fifty-person marketing company. Miriam charmed her interviewers' assistants. She conveyed a winning, sincere, and interesting personality during her office tour. Miriam did everything right. She was offered a job but didn't take it. Why? Because, based on her office tour, Miriam thought the company's atmosphere was quiet, boring, and stodgy. Wisely, Miriam realized that the firm was not going to be a good fit for someone with her energy level. Had Miriam never taken the tour, she would have been at a real loss when it came time to weighing the job offer. Miriam used the office tour to her advantage, effectively *controlling* her interview experience.

Everything we've covered in this chapter applies specifically to your interview process. If you think a little more broadly, though, our advice is really about two important things you've probably heard many times before:

1. You'll never have a second chance to make a first impression.

2. Treat everyone you meet with courtesy and respect, just as you would expect to be treated.

If you take this to heart, your dress and comportment will fall nicely into place, and you can stop worrying about this part of the challenge you're facing.

NO ONE REMEMBERS A RAMBLER

"So," said the interviewer, "I haven't really had much of a chance to go through your resume in detail. Why don't you tell me about yourself?"

That's not too tough a question, thought Guy; just relax and begin at the beginning. "Well, let's see. I was born in a small town in central Ohio. I'm sure you never heard of it. My mother was a housewife and my dad ran an auto parts store in the next town, about twenty miles away. Anyway, I went to the local grade school until I was eleven. Then my parents decided to enroll me in a private school, Saint Bartholomew, because they were worried that I wouldn't get a good enough education in the public schools. Well, they must have been right because I applied to seven colleges and got into all but one. Cornell. I don't know why they didn't take me, but it wasn't my first choice anyway. Ohio State was, and that's where I went..."

DON'T TALK YOURSELF OUT OF A JOB.

Forty-five minutes later, the interviewer raised his hand. "Mr. Mitchellson, I'm afraid we've run out of time. I have another candidate in the waiting room and I don't want to be rude and keep her waiting. Anyway, it was nice to meet you. We'll let you know in a couple of weeks if we want to have you come back for some more meetings with the team. You know your way out."

Guy never heard a word. Not from this company, or from the other three companies he'd interviewed with in the last two weeks. "What's the problem?" he agonized. "The interviewers seemed to like me. After all, they smiled a lot while I was talking. And I have a 3.4 GPA, for God's sake. Why aren't they calling back? I can't even make it to the second round."

Every candidate has to be prepared for the possibility of not getting a particular job. It happens to everyone, and more likely than not, it will have nothing to do with you. A better-qualified applicant comes along, a hire from within, the chairman's daughter. The best advice?

Shake it off and move on.

But when, like Guy, you find yourself consistently rejected by multiple employers, it's time to stop interviewing and reassess your approach. As hard as it may be to admit, you're likely not succeeding because you're doing something wrong. You need to find out what it is before you blow another interview.

In Guy's case, the answer's easy. He talked himself right out of consideration. His was a monologue, not an interview, and we can bet that when the interviewer heard "I was born . . ." in answer to the "tell me about yourself" question, his brain went into hibernation. Guy may be remembered, but only because he told his interviewer nothing and bored the crap out of him while he was doing it.

It's easy to think interviewing well is some arcane science and that only the gifted few can master it. Not so. It's nothing more complex than learning how to tell your story in a meaningful and compelling way. It's an exercise in blending content (what you say) with context (how you say it). In this chapter we focus on beginning the process of constructing your presentation. Think of it as learning your lines before a stage performance.

Interviews make people nervous, in some cases incredibly so. They tremble, sweat, sometimes even throw up. That's because people's number one fear is the prospect of making a speech to a roomful of strangers. Ironically, fear of death ranks second. Interviewing is the evil twin of public speaking. Why? Because in the candidate's mind, the stakes seem so high. Win, and it's a job, a paycheck, and the comfort of being accepted as part of something important. Lose, and you face rejection, embarrassment, perhaps even humiliation.

But ask a candidate what specific aspect of the interview process causes the most fear, and the answer is almost always the same. "I'm terrified they'll ask me a question I won't be able to answer."

Think about that for a second. What question could an interviewer throw your way that you aren't capable of answering? The person interviewing you has never seen you before and has no information about you other than what appears on your resume. So where do you think these impossible questions are going to come from? Your resume, of course. And who wrote it? We hope you did.

So let's start by talking about how to create effective answers to the most common interview questions. Have you ever heard the expression "Don't reinvent the wheel"? It simply means, don't start from scratch. And it's the mistake most inexperienced and unprepared interviewees make as they attempt to respond to even the standard, meat-and-potatoes questions. In so doing, they add immeasurable anxiety to the process and usually come up with answers that end up sounding pretty lame.

Let's say you have two interviews scheduled in one day. In the first, the H.R. executive asks, "So I see you went to Scripps. What was that like?" You nervously cobble together what you hope is a satisfactory answer. Something about the great time you had, the courses you took, your major. Blah, blah, blah.

Two hours later you have another interview. Different company, different job opportunity. First question. "Tell me three things you got from your college experience."

You panic. "Three—ohmigod."

"Ummm, let's see. I guess I made some pretty good friends, that's one. I got a good education [pause] and, oh, yeah, I met a lot of people from different backgrounds."

"Whew, that was close," you congratulate yourself. "I almost blew it."

Well, to us, you *did* blow it. First, you didn't recognize you were being asked the same question in both interviews. So in each case, you came up with two different answers. Worse, you had to invent them on the fly. The result? Your responses showed little thought, told the interviewer practically nothing, and made you sound like everybody else. And as an additional reward, you scared the hell out of yourself doing it. There's a better way.

Over the years we've prepared candidates for thousands of interviews of every type. What do they have in common? In almost every case, the bulk of the questions tend to fall into one of four subject areas:

1. Education

2. Work experience

3. Strengths and weaknesses

4. Why you want the job

If you know in advance that 95 percent of the questions asked will be based on these categories, you'd be crazy not to have some damn good answers burned indelibly into your brain long before you ever step into an interviewer's office.

This is not to suggest that every question you'll ever get will be drawn from these areas. An interviewer might give you a problem to solve. "How would you go about calculating the number of Ping-Pong balls that would fit in a Boeing 747?" Or a behavioral question. "Tell me a time you let your teammates down." If you get thrown a question like this, the best advice we can give is take your time, keep your wits about you, and think before you answer. Remember, these questions are often designed to throw you off guard, so there's nothing wrong with taking a moment before you start talking.

THE SEARCH FOR THE PERFECT ANSWER

Understand something right at the outset. There's no such thing as a perfect answer. There are only good, bad, and mediocre ones. Let's say you're interviewing for an entry-level position in a commercial real estate firm. The interviewer asks, "Where do you see yourself professionally in three years?" A bad answer: "Well, I see myself working for a couple of years and then enrolling in business school and getting my M.B.A." If you were the interviewer, what would your reaction be? How about, "How could anyone be dumb enough to say that? Why should I hire him? He's gone in two years." End of interview, end of opportunity. (We didn't make this answer up. We hear it a lot.)

A mediocre answer is any response that doesn't send a positive message about you. It's not wrong, it's just a wasted opportunity. For instance: "I'd like to get my real estate license and ultimately end up in a supervisory position in some commercial development company." You've told your interviewer that you want to work in the real estate industry, something he probably already knows, and that you're ambitious enough to want to get promoted over the next few years. Big deal—so does every other candidate being interviewed.

> **CONSIDER WHY YOU ARE BEING ASKED A QUESTION AND WHAT THE INTERVIEWER MIGHT BE LOOKING FOR.**

Now for a good answer. "Well, if I were lucky enough to be offered this job, I would hope that in three years I could be managing a portfolio of development properties for this company."

What has this answer told the interviewer about you that the others hadn't? First, you've flattered the company by acknowledging the quality of the position you're applying for. Second, you've let them know you're ambitious. Nice, but not a deal-closer. Third and most importantly, you've implied you see your future with that company. That you just might stick around long enough for them to get some payback for spending fortunes training you. In a world where young people change employers as many as nine times before their thirty-fifth birthday, that's persuasive stuff.

Here's the point. The difference between a good and a bad answer is simply the kind of signal it sends to the person asking the question. Good signals, good answer. Bad signals, bad answer. Simple, isn't it?

THINK HEADLINES, NOT ANSWERS

How do you go about constructing the kind of responses that send positive messages to your interviewer? Think like an interviewer. If you're asked, "Talk to me about college," do you think your interviewer is sitting on the edge of his seat waiting to hear a twenty-minute recap of your educational career? We don't think so. He wants to know what you learned from the experience as a whole. Of course you made great friends—everybody does—but didn't it also teach you to function on your own? How about time management or problem-solving? Didn't you learn how to be a self-starter and how to function as part of a team? These are the qualities your interviewer cares about; this is what he's probing for by asking the question. So if you're talking about education, these become your key messages. Think of them as headlines in an ad. A good headline communicates the benefit of the product in a memorable way. A good answer does the same thing. We think this approach is more persuasive than talking about the fraternity you joined or your favorite professor.

Now let's talk about work experience. It's a sure thing you'll be questioned about your internships and/or summer jobs. It's the only way an interviewer can find out how you function in the real world. You have two choices. Option 1: you can repeat what's already been outlined in your resume by laboriously going over every job you held and what you did while you were there. A waste of time, we think. Option 2: you can communicate what your work history, taken as a whole, has meant. "As you can see, every job I've had has been in some area of communications. Writing, editing, story development, press relations. Not only did I gain valuable experience, I also learned I have a real passion for this business, and I know now that I want to make it a career."

You've now given your interviewer everything he needs to know about your four years of work experience and wrapped it up in a tidy, highly memorable package. Even the dimmest of interviewers won't escape your message.

It's likely the discussion of your work history won't end here. There'll be follow-up questions about your experience at this company or that, or specific duties on a particular job. Remember, the "key message" rule stays the same. *It's not what you did, it's what you learned.*

One final thought on key messages. The better you can relate them to the qualities required by the job you're seeking, the more powerful they'll be. Suppose you're applying for a position on the news desk of a local television station. Don't you think working under pressure and multitasking might carry more water than customer service and data analysis? Make sure you weave them in.

The most important thing to remember is that these "headlines" stay the same in every interview. Learn them well. They'll spare you the anxiety of having to invent a new answer each time. Big benefit. And you'll tell an interviewer something he's actually interested in knowing.

ALMOST EVERY JOB HAS VALUE

One of the most frequent complaints we get from our clients is something like "I cut lawns for the summer. What's that got to do with the position I'm applying for?" In fact, a lot. Did you handle money? Did you interact with customers? Did you sign up new clients? Each of these responsibilities involves a skill or a discipline that is valuable to almost any employer.

Did you work on a call desk for large phone company? Why isn't that a fabulous sales or customer service story? A counselor at a summer camp? Enormous responsibility, considerable people management/ leadership skills. Even collecting tolls on a turnpike can be turned into some kind of positive message about managing money and accountability. The point is, don't leave what you think are menial summer jobs out of your resume just because you don't feel they'll impress an interviewer. There's value in each of them. You may have to dig a little, but it's there.

DEMONSTRATE BY EXAMPLE

There aren't many hard-and-fast rules in interviewing. But here's one. If you make a statement during an interview about what you've learned or the kind of person you are, have an example ready to support the claim. If you say you're good under pressure, smart money says your interviewer will ask for an example. Make sure you have it readily available. Nothing looks more foolish than trumpeting about your stellar performance under pressure, only to have your interviewer watch you squirm while trying to think of an instance that demonstrates it. If you want to talk about how effectively you work in team environments (employers love this one), tell a teamwork story. It doesn't have to be too elaborate or momentous; just make it brief, clear, and to the point. Remember, examples give the claim credibility. Without them it's just boasting.

"WHAT ARE YOUR GREATEST STRENGTHS?"

Everybody hates this one. It makes candidates uncomfortable to talk about themselves in such a brazen, self-congratulatory way. But you can bet your new iPhone that you'll be asked something about your best assets.

Do yourself a favor. Avoid attributing qualities to yourself that can't be documented. A classic is: "I'm a hard worker." Maybe you are, but there's nothing on your resume that can confirm it. The same applies to "I'm organized," or our least favorite, "I'm good with people." First, almost everybody says them. They're the quickest way we know to guarantee your invisibility, or, as we say in advertising, to become wallpaper. Second, you have no way of demonstrating the truth of such claims. How can you come up with a persuasive example of your work ethic? Are you going to show a picture of your dorm room to underscore your penchant for organization? We don't think so. The message: avoid these claims; they buy you next to nothing. Following are some guidelines to keep in mind.

A GOOD ANSWER IS MORE ABOUT WHAT YOU LEARNED THAN WHAT YOU DID.

Cite strengths that can be demonstrated from your resume. We had a client who served as a paralegal for a law firm handling a highly visible civil suit. It had been covered for months in every newspaper and news broadcast. The stakes were enormous and the pressure intense. When this young woman said she was good in tight situations, we believed her. Everything about her resume screamed it.

Don't forget about your experience. We've listened to hundreds of candidates talk about what they perceive their best qualities to be. Almost all of them mention personal attributes, creativity, problem solving, etc., but almost none remembered to mention experience. If you're applying for a sales position and have held summer jobs or internships that involved selling, say so. It's an asset not everybody has. And it's of much more value to an employer than some fuzzy claim about your friendly nature or nose-to-the-grindstone work habits.

Choose strengths that are of value in doing the job. Interviewing for an analyst job? Talk about your comfort level with spreadsheets, your ability to extract meaning from pages of data. If it's a sales position you're after, talk customer service or the ability to close a deal. Ultimately these will resonate better than more general-sounding skills such as leadership or teamwork.

Be prepared with an example. We've said it before, but it bears repeating. While you're highlighting your strengths, don't be surprised if you're asked to provide specifics. "You say you are a good problem-solver. Can you tell me about a time when you used that skill, and what process you went through to arrive at the solution?" This is the kind of interview question that scares the hell out of the unprepared. You don't want to think up an answer to a question like this on the spur of the moment, so have one ready beforehand. You'll save yourself endless anxiety, and spare your interviewer the embarrassment of having to listen to you stumble through a poorly crafted response.

"SO BILL, TALK TO ME ABOUT YOUR WEAKNESSES."

This question gets asked in many ways. "You've told me what you're good at. What are you *not* good at?" Or, "If we hire you, what are we going to have to worry about six months down the road?" How's this for a ball buster: "If I called your former employer, what would he say your biggest problem is?"

If there's a question uniformly feared by job candidates, it's this one. On the one hand, you need to come up with a shortcoming that doesn't immediately turn off your interviewer. Now is not the time to confess how disorganized you are, how you leave everything until the last minute, or have anger management issues.

We've heard a ton of silly answers, but in our book, the hands-down winner of the stupid answer contest is, "Most people don't like me when they first meet me. It takes people a while to warm up." Answer the question this way and you can count on the fact that the next question you'll get won't be "So, when can you start?"

On the other hand, interviewers aren't stupid. At least some of them aren't. Don't think you'll get away with "I'm a perfectionist," or "I tend to be a workaholic." Any entry-level human resources manager will pick up on this kind of disingenuous response.

How do you choose a weakness that doesn't make you sound like a serial killer but that is credible and nonthreatening? Your answer is relatively unimportant. Most interviewers know whatever they get back by way of a response will likely be a load of crap.

Why do they ask it? Only because they think they're catching you off guard. It's their way of cleverly (they think) measuring how well you handle yourself in a pressure situation. Your challenge is to have a prepared answer, but make them think you've been ambushed. This is where a little acting comes in. "Boy, that's a tough question. [Pause and feign deep thought.] Hmmm, let's see. Well, I guess if I had to choose a weakness, it'd be that I get impatient when I feel I'm not being productive. You know, those three-hour staff meetings where nothing gets done and everybody feels they have to say something? They drive me crazy."

Interviewer to candidate: "Come on, are you telling me that's your only weakness?" Answer: "Probably not, but you kind of put me on the spot, so it's all I can think of right now."

This is a pretty good answer. You've played the startled-candidate card just right, chosen a weakness, particularly as it relates to a loathing for staff meetings with which everyone can identify, and haven't allowed yourself to be goaded into prolonging the negative discussion. Congratulations—you've escaped unscathed.

BE READY WITH AN EXAMPLE TO SUPPORT EVERY CLAIM YOU MAKE.

Some other good answers might be "I tend to take on too much responsibility," "I have difficulty saying no to my colleagues," or "Sometimes my desire to get along gets in the way of my leadership abilities." Again, these will be credible only if you come armed with examples.

Most importantly, answer the question and move on. Don't let your interviewer trap you into a twenty-minute conversation about your liabilities—unless, of course, that's what you want him to remember about you at the end of the interview.

There's another strategy for answering the weakness question that works wonders under certain circumstances. Let say you're painfully shy in interview situations. Your voice gets soft, you look down instead of making eye contact when you speak, your answers appear tentative and timid.

You can ignore the problem and hope that your interviewer won't notice. Be assured, he has. And he's likely made a mental note about your lack of self-assurance. Not exactly the impression you were hoping to make. So why not go on the offensive? "My greatest weakness? When people first meet me I can appear uncomfortably shy. But once they get to know me better, I'm very outgoing. My roommate tells me she can't get me to shut up."

Great answer. First, you've mentioned a problem the interviewer has probably already flagged. But now it's no longer an issue. Your acknowledgment has taken it off the table. End of problem. You even threw in a little humor. A classic case of what we mean by taking control.

We had a client who, when he got nervous, talked so loudly it made our ears ring. He didn't know he was doing it. When we told him, he thought we were kidding. We had to show him the tapes of his mock interviews. He was floored. What did we advise him to do? Choose his voice problem as his weakness. "You know, I'm told that sometimes when I get a little anxious, I tend to talk too loudly." Why was this a good choice? Because even though we'd temporarily convinced him to turn down the volume, we knew he would lapse back into his old habit. On his next interview, he was certain to blow the poor interviewer right out of the chair. Better to neutralize the issue by getting the problem out in the open and not letting it fester in the interviewer's mind.

Want to ace the "weakness" question? Follow these simple rules: One, have an answer prepared. Two, pretend you've been caught off guard by the question. Three, give a brief answer. Four, expect to be asked for an example and have it ready. Five, finish the conversation and move on. Follow this advice and you'll never get trapped by this question.

"SO, TELL ME WHY WE SHOULD HIRE YOU?"

It's a straightforward question. Almost every interviewer asks it. And almost every candidate blows it. Here's why. The natural inclination is to restate one's strengths. Bad mistake. For one thing, it's old ground, and your revisiting it isn't going to win any points. It was mildly boring the first time; it'll be annoying the second.

Listen to the question. Isn't the interviewer asking what sets you apart from all the other candidates applying for this job? What makes you different, better? Do you really think it's your work ethic or any of those other too-frequently-repeated attributes that make you stand out?

How do you answer such a question? How about this: "I know you've probably considered an enormous number of candidates for this job. It's a terrific position. And I'm certain that they all have credentials equal to my own. But what sets me apart is that no one you're talking to has more admiration for this company than I do. You have made yourself the undisputed leader in your category by outthinking your competitors and focusing on first-class customer service. I want to be part of this team. I'm not simply looking for a job, I'm looking for a job *here*."

> **"I'M NOT LOOKING FOR A JOB, I'M LOOKING FOR A JOB AT THIS COMPANY."**

What makes this such a powerful answer? First, you've acknowledged the quality of your competition and showed just the right amount of humility. Second, you've made a point of highlighting exactly what makes you different from other candidates, and you've done it in a way that flatters the company you're talking to. Remember, most employees are justifiably proud of where they work and the jobs they do. They're going to look to hire people who share that same passion.

One word of caution. Every time you meet with a different organization, you'll need to find some suitable justification that makes your passion credible. It's not enough to say, "I want to work here because you're a great company." Find specific qualities about the company that you respect or admire. "This company wrote the book on packaged goods marketing." Or, "You're a pioneer in the area of soft-tumor radiology." The point is that your enthusiasm has to have substance, should demonstrate your corporate knowledge, and should resonate with your interviewer. Be convincing. Otherwise it is just aimless flattery.

"SO, YOUNG MAN, TELL ME ABOUT YOURSELF."

Remember Guy Mitchellson? You met him at the beginning of this chapter. He was given this question and talked his way right out of a job offer. His mistake? Assuming his interviewer wanted an overview of his entire educational and professional career. Bad guess. The employer was really saying, "I'm too busy [read, "important"] to have studied your resume, so why don't you tell my why you're here." We call it the lazy man's interview question, and it strikes fear into the heart of every job candidate.

The answer is deceptively simple. Tell your brand story. "I recently graduated from [your college goes here] with a major in structural engineering and business. I'm hoping to get a job as an analyst for an international engineering firm that will benefit from my business and engineering background." Now stop talking. If your interviewer wants to know more he'll let you know. Maybe he'll ask why you chose that particular field, or why you didn't decide to practice engineering. In either case, answer the question only when and if it's asked. More questions but shorter answers make for more interesting and memorable interviews.

DO YOU HAVE ANY QUESTIONS?

This usually comes at the end of the interview, when the finish line's in sight. You've done a great job so far; don't blow it now. There are lots of good ways to answer such a question. "No thanks, I think you've told me everything I need to know" isn't one of them. Questions are an expression of your interest in the job and the company. So come prepared. A few do's and don'ts:

Don't ask questions that have no bearing on the job you're applying for. "What's the company's long-term marketing strategy for competing in Asian markets?" is a good example of a bad question. First, you're showing off and your interviewer will know it. Second, the person you're talking to probably won't know the answer, and even if he or she does, quite frankly, you're not an employee yet and it's really none of your business.

Don't ask a member of senior management to walk you through a typical day on the job. Honestly, they don't know. It's probably been twenty years since they've had the kind of job you're applying for. It may be important to you, but save these questions and others like them for people at more junior levels.

Don't ever, ever, ever ask about money, benefits, length of a workday, or vacations. If you're lucky enough to be offered a job, your new employer will provide you with an offer package outlining everything you'll need to know about salary, benefits, paid holidays, and vacation time. One caveat: these are usually non-negotiable. Remember you're an entry-level employee, not the strongest bargaining position. So, if you think the salary you're offered is too low, you always have the option of turning down the job. But spare yourself the embarrassment of trying to negotiate your way into a better employment package; it'll just make you look foolish.

Do ask questions that help an interviewer better understand the kind of employee you might be. One of our favorite questions is: "If I'm lucky enough to be hired, where do you expect I might be in three years?" First, it says you're ambitious and want to move up in the organization, music to any employer's ears. But most importantly, it signals your long-term interest in the company. As we mentioned earlier in this chapter, many young workers can have as many as six or seven jobs before they turn thirty, and the concept that you might be around long enough to pay back their investment in training you is a compelling argument. It will go a long way towards separating you from your competition.

Do ask to speak to other employees who have or have had the job you're being considered for. If you don't think you have a good feel for the job you're applying for, there's nothing wrong with asking your interviewer to let you talk to other people who have similar jobs. It's a reasonable request, and most employers will respect you for making it. Also, by talking to your potential colleagues, you'll unearth a lot of useful information about what it's really like to work for the company.

One last word of advice. Questions aren't measured by the pound. One good one is all you'll need. Remember, in interview situations, the type of question you ask is usually more important to the interviewer than the answer is to you.

Our advice on being a smart interviewee?

1. Think like your interviewer.

2. Develop your key messages beforehand.

3. Line up examples for every claim you make.

4. Show how much you want to work for the company you're talking to. Most interviews are painfully formal and awkward affairs. A little passion works magic.

5. Ask the interviewer questions that will showcase your commitment and passion.

AN INTERVIEW IS A SALES PITCH DISGUISED AS A CONVERSATION

Two similarly qualified candidates are applying for a job as a junior analyst for a boutique investment management firm specializing in the energy industry. Which candidate would you select? Let's look at their qualifications on paper:

Candidate 1

Name:	Todd Fletcher
Hometown:	St. Louis, MO
Education:	Economics and geology, Stanford University
Internships:	Summer internship with Texaco, Riyadh, Saudi Arabia; Summer internship with the U.S. Department of Energy, Washington, D.C.; Summer internship with Morgan Stanley, New York
GPA:	3.75
Interests:	Skiing, golf, soccer, rock climbing, jazz piano
Languages:	English, German, basic Spanish

Candidate 2

Name:	Sam Levinson
Hometown:	Phoenix, AZ
Education:	Economics and geology, Princeton University
Internships:	Summer internship with British Petroleum, Dubai City, UAE; Summer internship with Cambridge Energy Research Associates, Boston; Summer internship with Goldman Sachs, New York
GPA:	3.75
Interests:	Skiing, golf, tennis, hiking, Latin music
Languages:	English, Russian, basic Spanish

"Wow," you may think, "both candidates look phenomenal. How can I possibly choose between the two? I need to meet these guys in person. It's the only way I'll be able to decide."

Here's what happened. During the interview process, both candidates proved they had done their research. They answered questions well and solved problems accurately. But Sam Levinson landed the job. Why? Because throughout the interview process, Todd appeared formal, a bit stiff, and slightly arrogant. In contrast, Sam was easygoing, enthusiastic, passionate about the opportunity, and appeared ready to roll up his sleeves and dig in.

Sam won the job because he was the more *likable* candidate. He beat out the competition by approaching the interview as a sales opportunity. More importantly, he effectively closed the sale.

At Hayden-Wilder, we are continually asked, "What's the most important quality to convey in an interview?" Our answer: "likability." It stands to reason, if an employer is spending more time with his coworkers than with his family, he wants to hire coworkers he likes. After all, you can choose your employees, but you can't choose your family. It's much easier to spend late nights working on projects, or getting stuck in airports for hours on end, with someone you like. We know one corporate human resources manager who will only refer candidates who pass the "beer test." The candidate must be the kind of person with whom the supervisor can enjoy sharing a beer after work. According to this human resources manager, if the boss doesn't feel comfortable with the candidate in an airport pub, he should seek employment elsewhere.

> **LIKABILITY IS MORE IMPORTANT THAN QUALIFICATIONS.**

As marketing communications executives, we have run into situations like these for years. We've made many hiring decisions based on likability. With this as a gauge, decisions are easier to make, particularly if it's a simple tie-breaker between two extremely qualified candidates. It's more difficult when employers are faced with candidates who don't share the same qualifications. But ask any manager whether he would rather employ an impeccably credentialed candidate with zero personality, or a prospect with more modest qualifications but on outstanding personality. Likability wins every time.

The bottom line is, the hiring manager is looking for three key things when he makes a new hire: the ability to do the job, the ability to work well with the team, and the ability to reflect positively on the person who did the hiring. It's no wonder that likability is a key to the candidate's success.

"Fine," you may say. "I get the message. I'm a generally likable person, but I get nervous in interviews." Or, "It takes a while to get to know me. So it's hard for me to shine in an interview. There's no time to really understand my personality." We believe there are lots of ways to overcome this perceived barrier. You've probably heard from lots of friends, "Don't worry about it. Just think of it as a conversation." That's true, to a degree. But a conversation describes only the tone of the interview. Make no mistake about it: every effective interview also includes a sales pitch. In previous chapters, we've talked about great answers that help sell an employer on your personal brand assets, so you know you have the required information. It's now all about delivery.

We've all met salespeople we couldn't stand. You know the type. They're everything the stereotypical sleazy salesman can be: pushy, bragging, abrasive, loud liars who don't listen to a thing you're saying. It's no wonder you can't deliver an effective sales pitch if you're not likable.

Likability has become so important in the workplace that some universities have a mandatory social skills course to complete specific majors. Why? Because certain high-tech jobs seem to attract geeky propeller-heads who couldn't carry on a non-tech conversation if their lives depended on it. Corporate America is finding this type of behavior increasingly unattractive and distracting for other, more mainstream, employees. That's why Carnegie Mellon University in Pittsburgh requires all computer science majors to fulfill a requirement in social skills. These majors must accompany a friend to dinner, attend movies and cultural events, and study the art of conversation.

Delivering your sales pitch with warmth, humor, passion, and approachability are keys to your success. Sharing a likable personality, one that makes the employer comfortable, is often more important than your actual qualifications. Don't worry, we believe likability *can* be learned. It's a magic combination of your body language, tone of voice, manners, and pleasantries—and you'll be amazed at how easy it can be.

IS YOUR BODY LANGUAGE A PERFECT "10"?

Our research with human resources professionals and hiring managers uncovered some hysterical and some truly sad stories of candidates and their body language. It's amazing what can be communicated by your eyes, mouth, hair, arms, and legs. We've all seen animals communicate effectively with each other. It's done with body language.

Talk to the hand. Without saying a word, your handshake can make or break a first impression. Have you ever gone to shake someone's hand and ended up grabbing a bunch of fingers? It's soooo awkward. Your handshake should be strong and create a lock between the "V's" of your thumb and forefinger and the interviewer's thumb and forefinger. Don't vary your handshake for men and women. A firm handshake is appreciated by male and female

> **DON'T LET YOUR BODY LANGUAGE CONTRADICT WHAT YOU ARE SAYING.**

interviewers alike. Connect with your interviewer's hand for at least three to five seconds while you introduce yourself "Hi, I'm Joshua Alvi. It's very nice to meet you." Be sure your eye contact is straightforward and continuing throughout your introduction. Most people decide whether they are inclined to like someone within the first twenty seconds of meeting that person. The combination of a strong handshake and equally strong eye contact is a surefire way to exude confidence. Nobody wants to shake a weak, light, sweaty palm.

The eyes have it. In the first televised presidential debate, Richard Nixon lost to John F. Kennedy because of, among other things, poor eye contact. If you watch those black-and-white films, you'll see that Nixon's eyes were all over the place. The more he looked up or down, the more dishonest he appeared. You've probably been in a situation where you couldn't say anything and had to use your eyes to communicate. (Your rolling eyes said, "Can you believe she actually wore those leather pants?" Or, how about the time in the campus pub when your best friend encouraged you, through eye contact, to go talk to that pretty redhead.) Don't forget this valuable communications tool in an interview. Be careful, though: eye contact can work against you if you stare at the interviewer like a zombie. It's very unnerving. Like Nixon, shifting, darting, or downward-focused eyes convey dishonesty. On *CSI Miami*, you can always tell if the suspect is lying by watching his eyes. It's a dead giveaway. Use your eyes to communicate enthusiasm, passion, importance, empathy, humor, and interest to the employer. If you can make your eyes sparkle or be lively, use this to your advantage. It will go a long way in relaxing you and bring ease to the interviewer, making the overall interview experience enjoyable.

Face the truth. Your facial expressions can tell an interviewer a lot more than you want. We've trained many clients through videotaped mock interviews. The minute the little red light on the camera goes on, the majority of our clients look terror-stricken. This is certainly not a signal you want to share with a potential employer, particularly since you know all your subject matter and have a great brand story to share. Believe it or not, your facial expressions can completely contradict the information you are verbally imparting. We've all seen someone react to a question or situation like a deer in the headlights. We've also seen someone answer a question enthusiastically while facially projecting total lack of confidence. We remember our client

Alicia Katzman talking very positively about her camp counseling experience. But she contorted her face and looked so pained when she shared her story that she lost all credibility. It took showing her our mock interview tapes to prove it, but Alicia's frown disappeared instantly.

Facial expressions also can work to your advantage by conveying interest and emphasizing important comments or opinions. Your head also moves for a reason. Get comfortable turning your head to acknowledge someone who may be interviewing you while you're walking on an office tour. And don't hesitate to nod or shake your head to indicate agreement, disagreement, or amazement.

You wore braces for a reason. Straight white teeth. It's the American dream. It's part of the American image indelibly marked in the minds of people around the world. More than 80 percent of our clients wore braces on their teeth during their childhood years. You or someone close to you probably wore braces as well. Your parents spent a small fortune making your teeth straight, so take advantage of your pearly whites and *smile*. It's your biggest secret weapon. Candidates are often so worried about answering questions correctly that they forget to do it. We've had dozens of clients talk about what gets them excited about their accomplishments, while wearing a stone-faced expression. Smiling throughout an interview accomplishes several things: it shows the interviewer you are relaxed, it helps *you* relax, and it helps you project enthusiasm. Most importantly, a good smile shows a potential employer that you are warm, open, and friendly, which are desirable assets for all employees.

Is your posture perfect, or are you a poser? Here's where body language fitness really comes into play. Simply sitting up in your chair, however, isn't enough. We find that our clients who have played sports or danced are more likely to keep their shoulders square. Slumping is not an option. Neck straight; head high; chest open. Never cross your arms. It communicates one of three things: you're defensive, you're pompous, or you're disinterested. Put your hands on your lap or your thighs, and leave them there unless you are gesturing to make a point. Think of your yoga or Pilates classes and stretch to speak from your core. Great posture projects energy, confidence, and fitness, while poor posture communicates timidity, laziness, sloppiness, and introversion. And try to avoid sitting on a couch during an interview; it's a real posture challenger.

Hand-to-hand combat. Hand gestures can do one of three things: get the interviewer more involved in the story you are sharing, make you look like English is a second language, or make you look like a nervous idiot. Use hand gestures to emphasize a point: it was "enormous," it was so "frustrating," it was "perfect." Stay away from gesticulating throughout the conversation, as flailing hands are very distracting to watch. If you are a random gesturer and can't control your hands, simply fold them in your lap.

How annoying! Are you a pen clicker or spinner? Do you habitually unfold paper clips? Are you a business card flipper? We are constantly taking pens out of the hands of our clients. It drives us up a wall. Pen clicking is a distraction that can send an interviewer completely off course. Some of the smartest people in the world are pen clickers, but they're still annoying. If you know you love to click your pen, try using a felt tip with the cap off. We've had lots of clients who crack their joints when they stretch. If you love to crack your knuckles (or your neck, back, or ankles), resist the temptation and put your hands on the arms of the chair. If you know you slap your thigh for emphasis, don't. Again, keep your hands in your lap. Practice with your friends to see how long you can go without clicking, cracking, or slapping. Keep the interviewer's attention on *you*, not on your fidgeting.

You don't have to be drunk to be legless. Don't move your legs too much in an interview. Ladies, whether you are wearing a skirt or pants, it's always best to sit on the edge of the chair, with both feet planted firmly on the floor, knees together. If you are more comfortable crossing your ankles, that's fine, too. Put a picture of Queen Elizabeth in your mind (but forget the hat). Royalty always sit quietly and never cross their legs. It doesn't matter how great your legs are.

Men should also try to avoid crossing their legs in an interview, as nine times out of ten, it makes them sit too far back in their chair and conveys casual indifference. Keep your legs slightly apart and your feet on the floor so you can comfortably lean toward the interviewer if you are making an important point. Use your legs to support you and give you energy, rather than using them to relax and get comfy.

GETTING BACK TO THE CONVERSATION

We spoke earlier about being an effective salesperson while you interview. Picture in your mind the most successful salesperson you have ever encountered. It could have been the guy at the Apple store, or the woman at the Clinique counter, or the waiter who helped you order the best meal you've ever had. Chances are all these people exhibited the following qualities: honesty, sincerity, energy, good manners, and an understanding of your needs. In short, the most successful salespeople are good conversationalists.

A conversation is not a tennis game. It doesn't work like a rally: Whack. Question. Whack. Answer. Whack. Question. Whack. Answer. Yes, you're answering questions, but you're also working hard to get the interviewer to like you. So once you've headlined, nailed, and practiced all your answers to the most commonly asked questions, take a deep breath. Think about the question. Then think about the delivery.

Suppose the question is "I see you went to Syracuse. You must have frozen your butt off up there. Why don't you tell me what you got out of college?" Which answer do you think is better?

Answer 1:

"The three most important things I got out of college were the ability to solve problems, the opportunity to apply my technical knowledge to practical situations, and a love of data analysis."

While answer 1 is accurate, it's also robotic and lacks personality. Answer 2 does a couple of other, more positive things. It politely and humorously acknowledges the interviewer's comment about the weather in Syracuse, and it shows that the candidate is a human being. He talks about making friends. He proves to the interviewer that he not only listened to the question but also is attempting to start a conversation. He does this by using a "bridge" to get into the meat of his answer.

A bridge is exactly what it sounds like: a segue into the next phase of the conversation. Using bridges helps to establish the personality of the interviewee and build a relationship. How many times have you been at a bar and had a strange guy ask, "Hi. Can I buy you a drink?" If you're like most people, you'll think it's a pretty lame, overly direct request. But suppose the same guy had said, "Hi, I'm Stephen. It looks like you went to the game this afternoon, too. Would you like another drink?" Although it's still a lame approach, by building a bridge, Stephen was softer and made his offer less aggressive. You still might not accept the drink, but you probably would acknowledge that Stephen was attempting to make conversation.

It's important to establish a baseline of pleasantries in an interview, just as you would in any other sort of conversation. Why? Because by being pleasant, you can set the tone for the entire interview. It helps put you in control, even with the toughest and rudest of interviewers. Trust us, your effort to be pleasant is going to be noticed. You may not realize it, but the pleasant manner of your favorite salesperson really helped to make you more inclined to listen to what he had to say. It's the same thing in an interview.

Case in Point Our client **Klaara Angeles**, who wanted to get into couture fashion marketing, was fortunate to have a high-powered father who traveled in important business circles. When Klaara graduated and began networking for a job opportunity, her father gave her the names of several of his CEO colleagues. Klaara arranged an appointment with one of these contacts, Mr. Tuni, the chairman of a large luxury goods holding company. After the initial meeting, Mr. Tuni asked his senior human resources manager to meet with her. The minute the H.R. person entered the room, Klaara could feel the tension in the air. The H.R. woman sat down with a sigh, looked Klaara in the eye, and said, "You know, I don't usually meet with candidates at your level. You're just out of college, aren't you? I usually interview senior executives. I don't have much time, but our CEO asked me to meet with you."

Talk about making Klaara feel useless before she even had a chance to answer a question! Klaara paused, sat straight in her chair, and thought, *You bitch. What did I ever do to you?* Then she smiled, extended her hand, and said, "Hi, I'm Klaara Angeles. It's so nice to meet you. Mr. Tuni had wonderful things to say about you. I'm so grateful for your time." Instantly, the H.R. manager relaxed, apologized for her brusqueness, and began the meeting. Rather than a combative volley, the meeting was a pleasant conversation in which Klaara had a chance to effectively sell her experience and strengths. Klaara, through a combination of quick thinking, restraint, and the exchange of pleasantries, established control of the interview. The happy conclusion to the story is that the H.R. manager forwarded her resume to a prestigious fashion house, where Klaara is now a marketing assistant.

PARDON ME!

We continue to be blown away by stories of the bad manners interviewers witness in job candidates. Some of our own experiences are hall-of-fame material. The candidate who, like a squirrel, nibbled on a baguette from a bag in his lap throughout the interview. The candidate who put his feet up on the interviewer's desk. The candidate who pushed his food onto his fork with his finger and then licked his finger—about three hundred times in one meal. The candidate who ordered beers with lunch and then proceeded to tell dirty jokes. The candidate who coughed and hacked throughout the entire interview and never covered her mouth. The candidate who stepped into the elevator before his interviewer, let the doors close in her face, and then complained he didn't know what floor to go to for his meeting with her. We could go on and on.

Suffice it to say, bad manners, if exposed, can ruin your opportunity to land a job, especially if the job involves working with other people. And most do.

Companies, when hiring senior-level employees, often wine and dine the potential employee prior to making a job offer. It gives the employer a different perspective on the candidate and provides an opportunity to assess behavior outside of the office environment. Is the candidate comfortable in a more social situation? Can the candidate make polite conversation? Does the candidate know the correct fork to use? Can the candidate discuss business and eat lunch without talking with his mouth full? The ultimate question: Will I be proud of or embarrassed by this candidate if I sent him to dinner with a client?

More and more, companies are taking entry-level recruits out to lunch or dinner as part of the interviewing process, and with good reason. A business lunch is the ultimate test of likability and manners. So if you have the slightest question about whether you will stack up against the competition in the manners department, these tips are for you.

Hold the door. It is appropriate and appreciated if men hold the door for women. It doesn't matter if the woman is a peer, an underling, or the CEO; gentlemen should hold the door.

Give up the view. If you are seated at a table for two, and one seat has a view of the restaurant and the other a view of the wall or kitchen, take the seat with the wall view.

Use your napkin. The minute you sit down at the table, unfold your napkin and put it on your lap. There are no exceptions to this rule, even if the restaurant is casual and provides paper napkins. If you need to use your napkin during the meal, dab at your mouth; don't engulf the lower half of your face in a single huge wipe.

Pass the bread. If the bread basket is placed in front of you, pass it around the table before taking any yourself. If there is only one roll remaining when the basket comes back to you, leave it in the basket for someone else. You can live without bread, and the waiter will probably bring more anyhow. If you are provided a bread plate, place the bread and a pat of butter on the plate. When you eat bread, break off a single bite-size piece and butter it. Then eat it. Don't cut the bread in half, butter both sides, and take bites out of the halves. You'll look like a Neanderthal who's never tasted food before. And don't reach across the table to snare the bread, salt and pepper, or a condiment, even if it's only one person away from you. Ask the person closest to what you need. "Jorge, would you please pass the salt?"

Don't pig out. A corporate recruiter is taking you out to dinner with a couple of other seniors. You ask your classmates, "Are you going to pig out?" Most likely the answer is yes. Corporate recruiters laugh their heads off at the amount of food consumed by the college kids they entertain. Most recruits order multiple courses and the most expensive items on the menu. Stop and think about this behavior. Would you rather be characterized as a sane, polite candidate, or as a glutton who apparently has never eaten in a restaurant before?

> **MANY CANDIDATES PLAN TO PIG OUT ON THEIR INTERVIEWERS' EXPENSE ACCOUNTS.**

Stay sober. Never, *ever* order a drink at a luncheon interview. If your interviewer has a glass of wine with dinner, it is perfectly acceptable for you to have a wine or beer as well. But just one. Then move on to soda or water. There's nothing more pathetic than watching a sloppy, drunk candidate try to look sober at a business dinner.

Don't turn your soup into a Slurpee. If you are sure you don't slurp or make other annoying animal sounds when eating soup, feel free to order it. Be sure to use a soup spoon and move the spoon away from you, rather than toward you, when filling the spoon. Err on the side of leaving a little soup in the bowl when you're just about finished, instead of tipping the bowl to get the very last drop. Tipping the bowl is a pretty desperate move. When you're finished with the soup, rest the spoon on the plate underneath the soup bowl. Don't ever leave the spoon sitting in the empty bowl or cup.

Learn your forks. If you find yourself in a formal dining setting and are overwhelmed by the amount of silverware in front of you, remember one thing: use the utensils from the outside in. A salad fork(B, in the diagram on the following page) will be placed outside, to the left of the dinner fork(C). A soup spoon(F) will be placed outside, to the right of the teaspoon(E). A butter knife usually is placed on the bread plate(A), so be sure to use it (and not your dinner or steak knife) for your bread. Steak and dinner knives(D) always will be placed with the blade facing in. Fish forks are easy to recognize, as they have either flat and wide tines, or are very small. If there are two wineglasses at your place, the larger glass is for red(G), the smaller for white(H).

Watch your hands and mouth. Keep one hand on your lap at all times unless you are cutting your food. When you finish taking a bite, put the fork back on the plate. We've all seen people talk and wave their utensils around for emphasis. They look like gangsters. The same goes for knives. Once you have cut the piece of food you are going to eat, place the knife on the upper right-hand side of the plate, with the blade facing in. Then eat. Never talk with your mouth full; "show and tell" is for first-graders. If you are asked a question when your mouth is full, finish chewing and swallow before you answer. Your interviewer will be happy not to view the mush in your mouth.

Case in Point Likable candidates win time and again. Our client **Annie Plonski** graduated from a private women's college in the South, with a degree in American studies. Annie wanted to work in media sales, having interned at both an online company and a major magazine during her summers away from school. When Annie first walked into our office, our instant impression was, "No wonder this young woman can't find a job." She appeared aloof, imperious, and even rude. It turned out that Annie was afraid of being too friendly; she thought she needed to be superserious (read "haughty") when she was in "interview mode." Annie was worried that if she let her real persona shine through, interviewers wouldn't take her seriously. After working with Annie for a number of weeks, we were delighted to discover a smart candidate with a great sense of humor and a truly engaging personality. Once Annie realized it was possible to be both likable and taken seriously, she was a new person. She launched her career selling time for Disney radio and loves the client contact aspect of the job.

YOU CAN DO IT!

THE TIME HAS COME, AND YOU ARE READY

You're about to embark on one of the most exciting and anxiety-provoking experiences of your life—conducting the search for your first entry-level professional job. Looking for a job is an exhausting process filled with self-doubt, insecurity, and self-examination. It also can be wonderfully rewarding, and even exhilarating at times.

The good news for you is that you have a great plan, have practiced well, and are completely prepared for the game ahead. It's important you look at your search as exactly that—a high-stakes championship game. Think of all your resume and interview preparation as practice. Think of all your research as studying the opposing team's game tapes. Think of all your networking and sharing of your brand story as the beginning of the season. Now you're ready to get out there and win the championship.

STICK WITH YOUR PLAN

You've spent a lot of time putting your plan together; it's important you stick with it. Be patient. Nothing in this crazy job world happens overnight. You'll run into a lot of distractions that will try to steer you off course. Recognize a distraction when you run into one and stay focused. We've had clients who, after meeting one person, wanted to change the format of their resume, because the person they interviewed with thought it should be longer. No way.

Case in Point ➤ Parents also can be a distraction. Despite all your hard work, your parents may try to second-guess what you're doing. Our client **Blythe Cronin**'s mother phoned us several times because her daughter wasn't getting calls and e-mails returned. Mrs. Cronin decided the reason must be her daughter's resume, because she couldn't think of anything else. Mrs. Cronin would call us and lament, "It's been another day and no call-backs for Blythe. I think it must be her resume. I don't think people believe her accomplishments." How shortsighted of Mrs. Cronin. She hadn't even given her daughter two weeks to execute her plan. Surprise, surprise! After

Blythe began calling and following up with everyone she had contacted, she was able to arrange several informational meetings, which led to identifying real opportunities. With five weeks of hard work, networking, and follow-up under her belt, Blythe landed a terrific job in the medical technology business.

Case in Point ➤ Another classic distraction is the one our client **Matt Tedesco** ran into. He was presented with a job opportunity that wasn't part of his search strategy. Matt graduated from a major southwestern university with a double major in finance and marketing. He's a smart, likable, good-looking kid. He interned one summer in the marketing department at Frito-Lay and worked another summer in field sales for a big beer distributor. Matt wanted to get into product marketing with all his heart. He also wanted to move to the Northeast. After graduation, he spent the late

> **RECOGNIZE A DISTRACTION WHEN YOU RUN INTO ONE AND STAY FOCUSED.**

summer in New York City, pursuing opportunities with consumer products companies. Summer is probably the most difficult time to look for a job in New York, particularly in August. Lots of people are on vacation, commuters are tearing out of the city early to beat the heat and get to the beach, and the general mind-set is not as focused as it is during other times of the year. As a result, arranging networking and informational meetings can be challenging. Matt had given himself six weeks to land a job—a very ambitious summer goal. He was actively trying to arrange appointments, but they were coming in slowly. At the end of week four, a friend of the family called and offered Matt a high-paying but dead-end job in construction. Matt, who was dispirited and in a panic, accepted the position and moved back to Arizona. He's now trying to figure out how to start over again and focus on consumer products marketing.

The key lesson here? If Matt had stuck to his guns, he would have landed a job as soon as September rolled around. He was a terrific candidate and had a great story to tell, but he let his anxiety rule.

Don't allow yourself to be distracted by other job opportunities; you owe it to yourself to continue to pursue your intended career path.

IF ALL YOUR EGGS ARE IN ONE BASKET, MOVE THEM

Remember, the entire point of networking and sharing your brand message is to meet as many people as possible to help identify opportunities. It's important to keep the momentum going. Stay active. Don't put all your eggs in one basket by relying on a single job or a single company. The more at-bats you have, the more likely you are to hit a home run.

Case in Point Our client **Raffir Kazemi** graduated from an acclaimed techcentric university, with a civil engineering major and a marine engineering minor. Raffir was following his game plan, meeting lots of on-campus recruiters and networking with several outside contacts. One of Raffir's meetings went particularly well, and he was asked back for a second, then third round of interviews.

Raffir had a "great feeling" and "knew he was going to land the job," so he stopped moving forward with his plan and waited to hear from his number one choice. Three weeks passed and Raffir didn't hear a thing, despite repeated attempts to follow up with the company. And then the

> **DON'T WASTE TIME PSYCHOANALYZING YOURSELF OR BELITTLING THE EMPLOYER IF YOU DON'T GET THE JOB.**

e-mail arrived. It was a curt thank-you-but-no-thank-you. Raffir was devastated by the rejection. He had lost three weeks of time because he had put all his proverbial eggs in one basket.

Don't be a Raffir. Even if you are 99 percent sure you're going to land a position, keep on interviewing for others. That way, if your intuition pays off, you will be in the luxurious position of telling the people with whom you've scheduled meetings that you've already landed a job. Sweet.

NO NEED FOR A THERAPIST

If you don't get hired for a particular job, more often than not it has nothing to do with you. If you arm yourself with this knowledge, you'll save a lot of money on therapy bills. We know how easy it is to personalize and internalize rejections. It's human nature to ask yourself, "What did I do wrong?" Don't be discouraged; you probably did most everything right.

During our time in the marketing communications business, we must have disappointed hundreds of entry-level candidates who came to us and interviewed for a job. Why? For a number of reasons.

1. Perhaps the position was filled by an internal candidate. Many companies now require all job openings to be posted internally, to encourage hiring from within. This means that outside candidates compete with better-known, present employees.

2. We may have been facing a budget crunch and made the decision to wait to fill an entry-level position until funds were a bit less tight.

3. There might have been a situation in which we thought a present employee wasn't going to succeed in his job, so we interviewed candidates to replace him, but at the last minute the employee pulled a hat trick and we decided to keep him.

4. A client's daughter landed the job.

5. The chairman's nephew landed the job.

6. Another candidate simply had better qualifications.

In the majority of cases, the reason a candidate wasn't selected had nothing to do with him. (Unless, of course, he completely bombed, and you don't have to worry about that.)

Don't exhaust yourself by continually reexamining rejections. Don't waste time psychoanalyzing yourself or belittling the employer. Stay focused and move on.

FOLLOW UP WITH A VENGEANCE

Once you start contacting people, don't be like Mrs. Cronin and expect your phone to start ringing and your e-mail box to fill up. *You* are the person in control. *You're* responsible for managing communication between the contact and yourself. *Your* cover letter said you'd follow up, so be sure you do.

Use your best judgment walking the fine line between effectively following up and being a complete nudge. The people you are contacting are generally quite busy, so give them a chance to call you back. You'll be lucky to get a call back on the same day; usually it takes a few days. Likewise, one phone call from you every three to four days is enough of a reminder.

STANDING UP WHEN YOU LEAVE A VOICE MAIL WILL GIVE YOUR VOICE MORE ENERGY.

Keep your voice mails upbeat. There's nothing more exasperating than a long, drawn-out, monotonic voice mail from someone you've never met. Stand up when you leave a voice mail; it will give your voice more energy. Speak slowly and clearly, and be sure to leave your full name and phone number. Always say "thank you" at the end of the message.

If an assistant calls you back, don't worry about it. Remember what we said about assistants? They can either make it or break it for you, so be charming, friendly, and gracious. Ask the assistant if there is anything she can do to help you schedule a meeting. And be sure to say "thank you *so* much."

After you leave each meeting, write a few notes about what just transpired. Think about the qualifications the interviewer said he was seeking and the expectations he had. You can then use this information in your follow-up thank-you note. Also think about what you did well and what needed improvement, so you have something to work on for your next meeting. Then immediately update your contact database and move on to the next opportunity.

HAVE FUN

You're embarking on a new adventure and are completely prepared. Don't pressure yourself to the point of frustration. Instead, have fun with your search. You'll meet a lot of new, (mostly) interesting people. You'll have a chance to get a sneak peak inside companies you've always wondered about. You'll have the opportunity to determine if the chemistry feels right. And most important, after some hard work and perseverance, you'll be taking home a paycheck.

CONGRATULATIONS! YOU'RE HIRED

We know you'll be hearing those words shortly. Why? Because you've taken *control*. You've survived the incessant hovering of your helicopter parents by involving them in your search in a meaningful fashion. You've decided what you wanted to do and understood that the only way to land a first job is to be focused on what you can do for an employer, as opposed to the other way around. The brand story you developed is solid, compelling, and distinguishes you from the candidates competing for the same job. You've shared your brand story with the right people as you began your networking effort. The resume you wrote is terrific and is complemented by a cover letter that will make the reader want to keep reading.

Then you began to interview. You knocked people out with your research because you went the extra mile. You looked great, had *impeccable* manners, and everyone liked you. You definitely passed the "beer test." You may even have survived an adventure like our client Mariah Maloney, who, despite being panicked in New York during a snowstorm, made it to her interview on time. Mariah realized the subways and buses were hopelessly delayed and taxis were at a premium. She began walking from midtown to Wall Street, knowing she had to figure out a way to get downtown more quickly. Mariah sweet-talked a delivery service driver into taking her downtown to her interview. It cost Mariah $45, everything she had in her wallet, but it was money well spent. When she shared the story with her interviewer—who couldn't believe she was on time for the meeting—he was completely blown away. We don't recommend putting yourself in danger as Mariah did, but the point is that going above and beyond resulted in an invitation back for three more interviews, and she landed the job.

After several interviews, you really found your groove and started having fun. You knew the drill. In your mind, you were just waiting for the next question, to which you could respond with an answer that hit the ball out of the park. You followed up and followed up and networked and networked and followed up some more.

And then it happened. The offer came in, and they wanted you to start work the following week. Congratulations! You won the championship game. It's time to celebrate. And by the way, welcome to the first phase of a long and successful career.

ACKNOWLEDGMENTS

Many friends, colleagues, and relatives deserve our thanks for supporting us as we built Hayden-Wilder and wrote this book. Special acknowledgments go to:

Bob Borden, who had enough faith in us to allow his son Rob to be our first student at Hayden-Wilder • Chip Cipriani and Kathy Greer for providing help and design excellence when working with us to get Hayden-Wilder off the ground • Geline Williams, who believed in our concept from the get-go and continues to provide valuable, clear counsel, all wrapped-up in a gift of dear friendship • Camilla Rich, Jane Wykoff, Paula Gleysteen, Dana Billings, Beverly VanOrman, and all the other parents who trusted us enough to counsel their children and so enthusiastically recommended us to their friends • Jackie Herskovitz, our publicist, who understood what we were trying to do from the outset and worked so hard to get us press coverage any company might envy • David Hayden for his ongoing encouragement of our entrepreneurial efforts • Sandy Wilder and Janet Egan, without whose support Hayden-Wilder would never have seen the light of day • To Ted Raymond, a special thanks for putting a roof over our heads in our early years and for being such a staunch supporter of the Hayden-Wilder concept. • Nancy Mobley for her generous and enthusiastic support and counsel • Sarah Morton, who from the beginning, has been a tireless cheerleader and advocate for our book venture • Betsy Maling for taking care of Mosby during the writing, editing, and rewriting of this book • Kristen Latta, our editor, for her listening skills, guidance, and steady hand during the production of this book • Tim Horgan, for his patience and talent in making our Web site work for our business • Pauline Ahearne (and her amazing family), for her friendship, strong spirit of always pushing forward, and for watching Maeve, no matter the time or the weather • Rick Rota, for food, drink, humor, support, and understanding during the writing process • The Hayden-Wilder board of advisors, for their unfailing support of our business concept • Mel Parker, our agent, without whose vision and guidance this book would have never been written • All the entry-level employees with whom we've had the privilege to work.

ABOUT THE AUTHORS

D.A. Hayden, a partner in Hayden-Wilder, has more than twenty-five years of experience in integrated marketing communications. As a creative strategist for existing and start-up companies, she ensured strong, relevant marketing communications drove client business results. Her experience includes working with global, Fortune 500, start-up, and turnaround companies in the consumer, retail, B2B, financial, and service sectors. Her experience hiring and training employees at all levels led her to counsel college graduates in securing a career-building first job.

D. A. is a graduate of Manhattanville College and has completed graduate studies in broadcasting. She is an avid equestrian and holds board positions with several organizations that focus on land conservation and education. Her first job out of college was with a public relations agency in New York City. It paid $10,500 a year.

Michael Wilder is a partner in Hayden-Wilder and has more than thirty years experience in merchandising, promotion, marketing, and strategic planning in a variety of industries. His extensive background in building strong brands and managing teams of people translates to real-world expertise in guiding recent college graduates through the hurdles of a first-time job search.

Michael guest lectures and teaches branding at several New England colleges and universities. He serves a variety of not-for-profit organizations and currently serves on the board of trustees of Dana Farber Cancer Institute.

Michael holds a B.A. from Columbia University and was a lieutenant in the U.S. Navy. He is an active outdoorsman and avid fly-fisherman. His first job upon graduating from college was in the advertising business in New York City, where he earned $9,000 a year, with no benefits.